MW01627473

Eileen

The story of Eileen Jackson
as told by her daughter

JERRY WILLIAMSON

Foreword by Neil Morgan

San Diego Historical Society
in association with
KALES PRESS

Published by the San Diego Historical Society in association with Kales Press

Edited by Dr. Harry Polkinhorn, Director
San Diego State University Press

All photographs are from the author's collection except as noted

First Edition 2000

Library of Congress Catalog Card Number: 00-107101
ISBN 0-9670076-3-1

San Diego Historical Society
1649 El Prado, Balboa Park
San Diego, California 92101

Kales Press
7031 Columbine
Carlsbad, California 92009

Printed in Hong Kong

To Tom

Friends of Eileen Jackson

Benefactor

J. W. Sefton Foundation

Sponsors

Grace Bentley Allen
Marian and John Barry
Roberta and Malin Burnham
Elizabeth and John Carson
Patricia and Hugh Carter
Anne Evans
Justine B. Fenton
Dorothy and Al Frost Jr.
Jeanne and Gordon Frost
Audrey Geisel
Lyn and Philip Gildred
Alison and George Gildred
Connie K. Golden
Mary and Bruce Hazard
Jean and Keith Hollenbeck
Elizabeth Hubbard
Renee and William Jenkins
Philip M. Klauber
Joy and Merl Ledford
Karon and Gordon Luce
Nancy and Peter Peckham
Kay and David Porter
Dr. Norman C. Roberts
Donna Sefton
Dori and Craig Starkey
Marian Trevor
Dorothy Tyson
Barbara Walbridge
Ginger and Robert Wallace
Gerald Warren
Betty Jo and Hal Williams

Friends of Eileen Jackson

Contributors

Betty and Arthur Austin
Mrs. Betty Bass
Arthur Bell
Judy and Scofield Bonnet
Barbara Cole
Helen Copley
Mary Isabelle and Howard E. Crofts
Alex and Betty Debakcsy
Ruth and William Dick Jr.
Jinx Ecke
Doris and Peter Ellsworth
Mary Fadem
Jane and Thompson Fetter
Joy and Fred Frye
Nancy Garland
Abbie and Don Giddings
Alyson Rice Goudy
Gordon Reeve Gould
Louise and Richard Haugh
Eleanor and Arthur Herzman
Barbara and Frank Hope
Aline G. Hornaday
Rebecca J. Irwin
Nancy and David James
Catherine T. James
Norma and Oliver B. James
Linda and Payne Johnson
Rosalie B. Kew
Lael and Jay Kovtun
Klonie and Frederick Kunzel
Joanne Lambert
Patricia Lester
Margaret Cary Lieb
Barbara and Edgar Luce
Margaret and Arthur Marston
Virginia W. Martin
Alice K. Miller
Patricia and George Molyneaux
Judith and Neil Morgan
Judith and Walter Munk
Kay North
Lee and Peter Norton
Elsa M. Pettit
Ord Preston
Victoria M. and RAdm. Haley Rogers
Lois and Donald Roon
Kathleen Arnold Scales
Jerrie and Jim Schmidt
Mary Louise and John Shoemaker
Christine and Fred Stalder
Stanford Steinbeck
Janet Sutter
Ruth and Robert Swisher
Letitia H. Swortwood
Mrs. Marjorie Claire Tavares
Marcia M. Thaxton
Mary Jane and James Wiesler
Patricia and Donald Worley

Contents

Introduction by Robert M. Witty 11

Foreword by Neil Morgan 13

Preface 15

A Ramona Childhood 19

The Cub Reporter 27

Marriage 41

Social Reporting During the Depression 53

On the Eve of War 67

The War Years 81

Some Tricks of the Trade and a Surprising Move 89

The Journal Years 97

Battling Leisure 131

Washington, D.C. and San Francisco 141

Following the Queen 151

Work and Play 161

The Pack Rat and Questions of Etiquette 173

Four More Conventions and Europe at Last 185

A Kind and Hard-Working Galley Slave 195

Countdown to Retirement 209

Retirement—For a While 221

Adelante por Atrás 235

Honors and Celebrations 249

Last Years 257

Introduction

Jerry Williamson has written a loving and lively biography of her mother, Eileen Jackson, who chronicled the city's social activities for 60 years as a newspaper columnist.

Eileen, as she was known to partygoers, readers and colleagues, held a special spot in San Diego journalism. She dug beneath the exterior of the social scene for the substance of the people and events she covered, and created an epic spanning several generations.

The author does not ignore her father, Everett Gee Jackson, who was at Eileen's side for 69 years. A respected artist and professor of art at San Diego State University, he wrote his own memoirs in four illustrated volumes.

The San Diego Historical Society is publishing "Eileen" in an association with Kales Press; an earlier collaboration produced the stunning Donal Hord Catalogue for the 1999 Hord sculpture exhibition at the museum.

We are grateful to Eileen Jackson's many friends whose generosity has made this publication possible. Special appreciation is due Kay Porter, Donna Sefton, Anne L. Evans and others on the Steering Committee. The Steering Committee included Elizabeth Carson, Barbara Cole, Mary Fadem, Betty Hubbard, Barbara Luce, Dorothy Tyson and Barbara Walbridge. A special thanks also go to the J. W. Sefton Foundation. The Friends of Eileen Jackson are listed in the front of the book.

Eileen's portrait on the cover is the work of Antony di Gesu, who photographed many famous personalities from his base in New York. After moving to San Diego, he recorded on film most of the movers and shakers in this city in the 1960's and 1970's. Eileen's portrait is reprinted with the permission of his widow, Alice di Gesu, who has donated his extensive negative and print collection to the San Diego Historical Society.

— Robert M. Witty, Executive Director
San Diego Historical Society

Foreword

Eileen Jackson, in white gloves and hat, was the social mentor for a young city through three generations. Her writing—her straws in the wind—was gracious but demanding. With it, through sixty years, she invested San Diego with a hierarchy of her own invention and made it real.

When family and personal decisions needed making, each generation of friends and readers came at some time to ask themselves the question: "What would Eileen think?" A serious number of proposed marriages were not announced without anguished concern about how Eileen would view the match.With such personal force, Eileen came to create a part of San Diego life as reliably as Herb Caen created San Francisco each day in zinger items.

As the indefatigable social reporter, Eileen took me along to my first San Diego Charity Ball when Mrs. Henry B. Clark still held court.

The Charity Ball was the annual summit of the social rituals that Eileen defined, an evening when social caste ruled, and the presumptuous came unglued. Eileen adored it. She pretended not to dote on the stars of her San Diego cast, but everyone watched as Eileen moved from box to box and somehow managed to report what almost everyone wore and with whom they wore it.

Mrs. Clark (I never ever risked calling her by any other name), was a persistent and imposing woman who had chaired the first Charity Ball in 1909. Lena Sefton Wakefield Clark lived so long that she returned in triumph as chairwoman of another Charity Ball four decades later. Eileen, the unchallenged historian of the balls, wasn't old enough to attend a Charity Ball until 1924. By 1949, at the peak of her newspaper game, she absolutely smothered Mrs. Clark's encore ball with her coverage.

On the weekend of the 1995 ball, Everett Jackson, at 94, checked into Mercy Hospital. The next day Eileen, then 88, joined him at the hospital for exploratory surgery. These two always did everything together.

They had even became Mr. and Mrs. San Diego together, in 1992. I remember talking to Eileen at Mercy Hospital during that stay, and, a dogged reporter to the end, she said she'd had to miss the ball. Jo Bobbie (Showley), she said, had told her it was lovely but a lot of people she was accustomed to seeing at Charity Balls weren't there. Eileen said she'd had to remind Jo Bobbie that they were getting old.

That was not true, not for any of us who knew Eileen and could see nothing but that all encompassing young smile.

In this charming chronicle, you will find precisely what all of us who loved Eileen have needed for a triumphant keepsake of her life. Few people have left a more beneficent mark on this city than Eileen and Everett. They live on through that, and through the pages of this book.

—Neil Morgan

Preface

At nighttime when I was a child, I often fell asleep to the sound of a typewriter. It came from my parents' bedroom across the hall. When I was a year old, my mother said to my father, "The baby will just have to get used to it," and get used to it I did. For years the soft tapping sound of my mother's typing soothed me at night. It was my reassuring lullaby.

My mother, Eileen Dwyer Jackson, was an unrepentant career woman long before most women had ever thought of seeking high-powered jobs outside the home. Her newspaper career began when she was twelve and continued, with a few time-outs, until she was eighty-four. She identified with her hometown, San Diego, California, and she became its premier social scribe. Some people felt she limited herself by sticking so close to home. When she ventured beyond her hometown in the 1950s, to cover a political convention and to follow a queen on tour, several of her reporter friends from the Washington, D.C., and New York papers urged her to leave San Diego. They assured her that she had what it took to shine at the national level.

"You're good enough to compete with the best reporters in the country," one East Coast newswoman told her.

"Yes," said another, "and as proof of that, sometimes you've even scooped us! You don't belong in that little California town."

My mother laughed when she heard those words. If she left San Diego, she said, she would have to desert "her people," her beloved family of readers. To Eileen, her San Diego audience was the only one that mattered. She might be a top-flight newshen, and recognized as such by her peers, but she was a mother hen where San Diegans were concerned. She fussed over them; she wrote up their births, weddings, and benefit balls, and she entertained and educated them with her weekly editorials. For years her warm voice on the phone announcing, "This is Eileen" had brightened the mornings of countless San Diegans. They had told her so, and they were the people she knew she could never leave.

Although Eileen laughed at many things, including the suggestions of her East Coast reporter friends, one thing she didn't laugh at was the women's movement. She applauded it; she felt it was a movement whose time had come. Yet one aspect of it perplexed her. There were no roadblocks and no villains in Eileen's world. When she was a girl, it never occurred to her that she couldn't become a reporter on a major newspaper someday, and a star reporter, at that. She didn't believe that men would try to hold her back, but if they did try, if they were so silly as to think they could rein her in, she knew they would never succeed.

Eileen was a dynamo, an adventurous woman whose natural inclination was to look ahead and to move ahead. She welcomed the challenges she encountered in her career and tackled them with confidence. I think she sometimes wondered why the feminists talked so much about the barriers women faced. The Nike Company's slogan could have been my mother's: "Just Do It!"

As a child, in the 1930s, I was aware that the mothers of most of my friends stayed home each day and "kept house." A typical little girl of that time did not fall asleep at night to the sound of a typewriter, nor did she go downtown on school holidays to visit her mother's office. I knew my childhood was slightly unusual, but I wasn't bothered. There were always plenty of adults around to care for me—two devoted grandparents, a succession of kindly housekeepers, an artist/college-professor father who arranged his class schedule so that he could leave early each afternoon to pick me up at school. I never felt neglected, and I didn't resent my mother's career. I accepted the fact that she wrote for a newspaper. I couldn't imagine her doing anything else.

Because my mother was a pioneer of sorts, and because she accomplished so much in her lifetime, I felt that I should tell her story. A knowledgeable friend encouraged me to write this biography, but advised me to stand back a little from my subject, to keep some distance between us for objectivity's sake. I thought that was good advice. I hoped that each time I referred to my mother as "Eileen" in this book, I was creating some distance. But then I would have referred to her as "Eileen" anyway—and to my father as "Everett"—for I had always called my parents by their first names.

For six months after Eileen's death, I immersed myself in her papers. And they were definitely her "papers," not her "files." I am not talking about alphabetized manila folders containing neatly trimmed newspaper articles. My mother was a creative genius, and a woman of many virtues, but she was not neat. Besides, she was always busy writing her next column. She didn't have time to cut out yesterday's articles and file them.

She did save her columns, however—not all of them, but a great many. She also saved her feature and travel articles, her editorials, and the letters people had sent her. In a haphazard fashion she filled the drawers of her home office with papers, and she stuffed papers into her dresser drawers, into both big and little boxes, into suitcases, and even up among the hats on her closet shelves. I learned that it was all there somewhere. Sometimes she wrote grocery lists on papers that she knew ought to be saved, so of course she saved those papers, too.

I found one charming personal note to her from Senator Barry Goldwater, written on U.S. Senate stationery. "Dear Eileen," it began. At the bottom of the page, beneath his signature, my mother had scribbled the words "buttermilk, radishes, sour cream, enchilada sauce, coffee." But she cherished the senator's letter, so it joined others like it in the dresser drawer.

I went through all those drawers, boxes, suitcases and shelves, and I cut out her articles as a child might cut out paper dolls—lovingly, carefully. Many of the newspaper pages were yellow with age, and many of them were as delicate as old lace. I put Scotch tape on the back of some of her articles, to hold them together, and I put everything into neat manila folders. Then I began to find notebooks and journals in which she had reminisced about her adventures as a newspaperwoman and about some of the celebrities she had interviewed.

In telling Eileen's story, I have used her words as well as my own. I have quoted extensively from her editorials, columns and reminiscences. I like to think that my mother and I have collaborated on this book, that together we have chronicled the life of a most amazing woman.

A Ramona Childhood

Throughout her adult life, Eileen used to tell people, "I grew up in Ramona. That's where I spent my childhood."

In truth, Eileen spent only two years in Ramona, a rural community about forty miles northeast of San Diego. It loomed large in her memory because it was the place where she experienced both the happiest and the most frightening moments of her childhood. But the happy moments were the ones that colored her view of Ramona. Even though she suffered a terrible accident toward the end of her stay there, she always considered it a special place.

Eileen Lois Dwyer actually lived the first ten years of her life in a city. She was born on Easter Sunday, April 15, 1906, in San Diego, California. The population of San Diego at the time of her birth was around thirty thousand.

She had an unusual genealogical heritage. On her mother's side, the Morse side, she was descended from the early Puritan settlers. She was a direct descendant of many illustrious early colonists, including Thomas Welles, Governor of Connecticut Colony in 1655 and 1658. Eileen's Morse great-grandfather, a New Englander, came to San Diego by train in 1888. He brought with him his entire family—his wife and his grown, married sons and their families.

Eileen's father, on the other hand, was of Irish descent. His father, Jeremiah Dwyer, left Ireland for America in the late 1850s. After fighting for the Union in the American Civil War, Jeremiah wandered out to St. Paul, Minnesota. There he met and married a young Irish-Canadian woman named Mary Lawless. The married couple gradually made their way west to

Virginia City, Nevada. Eileen's father was born in that little silver-mining town in 1876, at the time of the big bonanza. A few years later Jeremiah and his family moved to northern California. Then, in 1886, they migrated south to San Diego.

Eileen's parents, Vera Morse and Edward Dwyer, were married in San Diego in 1905. My father used to say that his mother-in-law's Puritan genes and his father-in-law's Irish ones must have combined in a strange and wondrous fashion to produce a creature like Eileen.

Three days after she was born, the San Francisco earthquake occurred. The family story has it that my grandmother was so interested in the earthquake news she ignored her baby for several days and did nothing but read the newspapers. The family believes Eileen decided right then that if she was going to get anyone's attention in life, she would have to become a newspaper reporter.

Eileen was a beautiful baby. She had Irish coloring—black hair and blue eyes—and delicate features. She weighed only five pounds at birth, but she caught up fast once she regained her mother's attention, and she grew more beautiful every day. She was, in fact, beautiful all her life.

As a child, though, she was a handful; she was wild as well as beautiful. She always wanted to dash out into the street, or to climb that far-off mountain. Her mother, in desperation, made a kind of harness for Eileen and put her on a leash when they went walking. Strangers criticized my grandmother.

"You are treating your child like a puppy," they told her.

"No," she informed them, "I am trying to save her life!"

Eileen's brother, William Newton Dwyer, was born one year after Eileen. Their personalities couldn't have been more different. When Bill was little, he was shy and quiet. Distant mountains did not interest him, nor did dangerous streets. He didn't need a harness. He was loving and loyal, however, and he and Eileen remained close all their lives. When he died, at age eighty-eight, he left his children property and money, but no personal papers. He left no letters, no notebooks, no journals—

as his daughter said, "No paper trail at all." Clearly, my Uncle Bill was very different from my mother.

*

In 1916 the family moved from San Diego to a small ranch in Ramona. My grandfather, who was a building contractor, wanted to try ranching for a change. He also wanted his children to live in the country. They were ecstatic. They now had fruit trees to climb and animals to play with. Upon moving to the country, their parents had acquired a horse and cow, a goat, and some chickens and ducks.

Eileen and Bill attended a one-room school, the Earl School, during their years in Ramona. There were seven children in the school, representing almost that many grades. The first teacher they had was "mean and old" (Bill's description of her seventy-nine years later). As they reminisced about her in 1995, neither Eileen nor Bill could remember the teacher's name. But they did recall an incident that had taken place in the schoolroom seventy-nine years before.

Apparently Eileen had decided that that mean teacher was favoring the richer children in the school and was treating the poorer children harshly. On the financial scale Eileen and Bill fell in the middle, so Eileen was not thinking about herself when she brought this issue up. All her life she would become furious whenever she felt an adult was mistreating a child.

One day the teacher lost her temper and began shaking one of those poorer children. Eileen ran up to her and told her to stop. The teacher then grabbed Eileen and began shaking *her*. At that, Bill ran across the room and started pummeling the teacher. "Stop shaking my sister!" he screamed.

"That teacher was so mad at me," he told his family in 1995, "that she refused to promote me at the end of the school year. She kept me back. But the next year Miss Lovejoy became our teacher. She was only about eighteen years old, and she was sweet and pretty. At the end of that second year, *she* promoted me *two* grades, so when I went back to San Diego to school I was right where I belonged!"

*

When Eileen was eleven, a great troop of soldiers marched to Ramona. Years later Eileen told her granddaughter about the day the soldiers arrived. They were preparing to go and fight in France, and the march was part of their training.

Everyone in Ramona seemed to have heard about the march. People lined the road and waited for the soldiers to appear. Eileen and Bill positioned themselves on a large rock next to the road.

Finally the crowd could hear the sound of marching feet in the distance. Then the men came toward them, hundreds of men, it seemed to Eileen. She quivered with excitement and tugged on her long black braids. The men came closer—and closer. Suddenly they were marching directly in front of Eileen and Bill. One of the soldiers looked over at Eileen and said, "Hello, sweet cookie!"

Eileen fell off the rock.

*

By the time Eileen was twelve, she knew what she wanted to be in life. She had thought it over and had made a decision. She wanted to be a newspaper reporter.

She had written stories and poems for years, but at age twelve she sensed that going after a story about real people and real events might be more exciting—and more fun—than making something up. Fiction writers sat in little rooms, all by themselves, and wrote. Newspaper reporters, on the other hand, went out into the world and talked to people before they did their writing, and Eileen liked to talk to people almost as much as she liked to write.

Now that she knew what she wanted to be and do in life, she thought she'd better get started. Never one to wait around after an idea had entered her head, she hurried to the office of the

Ramona Sentinel, the little local paper. She walked in, introduced herself to the editor, and announced to him that she would like to write up the social news of her area for the *Sentinel*. The startled editor said that he didn't think that part of Ramona, a farming area, had any social news. Eileen assured him that it did. Like so many men after him, the editor succumbed to her persuasiveness. He said that if she could find some social news in her district, and if she wrote it up, he would print whatever she had written.

Eileen ran out of the office to look for some news. Soon she was contributing items to the *Sentinel*. Her newspaper career had begun.

*

Eileen's mother was a Christian Scientist, and she raised her children in that faith. My grandfather had drifted away from the Catholic Church as a young man. Although he still respected the Catholic religion, and in some ways still identified with Catholics, he made no objection when his wife told him that she wanted Eileen and Bill to grow up as Christian Scientists.

In the summer of 1918 Eileen was in an accident that involved a runaway horse. She was so badly hurt that even her Christian Scientist mother agreed she should go to a hospital.

Eileen was sitting in a little horse-drawn buggy one day, waiting for her father to come out of the house so they could go for a ride. Suddenly a flying piece of paper startled the horse. In an instant it took off down the road at a fast gallop. Eileen fell partway out of the buggy and somehow got her left leg caught in the spokes of one of the buggy wheels. The horse ran only a short distance, but by the time the skittish animal came to a stop the turning wheel had completely mangled Eileen's leg. Her parents had heard her screams. They ran after her and pulled her from the buggy. Her father placed her on a mattress in the back of a truck, and her mother climbed in beside her. Then they hurriedly drove to a hospital in San Diego. When they reached the hospital, the mattress was soaked through with blood.

The doctors in the hospital examined Eileen's leg. After a

short consultation they informed her parents that it would have to come off—and right away. By then Eileen's mother had called in a Christian Science practitioner. My grandmother pleaded with the doctors to wait until the next morning before amputating Eileen's leg. After discussing the situation, they reluctantly agreed to postpone the surgery.

"Those bones have been smashed to pieces," one doctor told my grandmother. "They will never knit."

"We'll see," she said.

She and the practitioner remained with Eileen all night. When the doctor arrived at the hospital the next day, he found, to his surprise, that the bones in Eileen's leg *had* begun to knit. A short while later he told Eileen's parents that her leg would not have to be amputated after all, that although she would have a badly scarred leg all her life, it would be a usable one.

"But," he added, "I can't understand how those bones started to knit like that!"

Eileen's mother said nothing; she merely smiled. The knitting ability of Eileen's smashed bones didn't surprise my grandmother at all.

*

Later that summer the Dwyers moved back to San Diego. After Eileen's father got the family settled in a new house, he resumed his career as a contractor. He had moved back at the right time. Eventually he built many of the large Spanish-style homes that appeared around town in the 1920s.

That fall of 1918, Eileen started the eighth grade at a grammar school in San Diego. The country interlude was over. For Eileen it ended with a shattered leg, but in spite of the accident she always remembered those years in Ramona as the happiest years of her childhood.

Eileen did have a badly scarred left leg for the rest of her life, and she also had a slight limp. But the leg didn't keep her from chasing after stories (and getting them before anyone else), or from dancing, or from climbing Mayan pyramids with her husband. People rarely noticed her bad leg. Most people couldn't take their eyes off her beautiful face.

In the late 1970s Eileen met two middle-aged women at a luncheon in San Diego. They told her that they had lived in Ramona all their lives. Eileen started to explain to them about her Ramona childhood when one of the women said, "Oh, we know who you are. Before you retired, we used to read your column every day. But we've always known about you in Ramona. You were the 'miracle girl,' who was in that accident. Tell us, are you still a Christian Scientist?"

"No," Eileen said. "Well, sort of, but I don't go to church anymore, or 'read the lesson' and that kind of thing."

"Well, *we* are Christian Scientists," the woman said. "Didn't you know? A whole bunch of your neighbors in Ramona became Christian Scientists after your leg was saved. Our mothers became Scientists, and raised us in the Church. And it was all because of you!"

The Cub Reporter

Eileen entered San Diego High School as a freshman in 1919, when she was thirteen years old. She still had the look of a country girl. With her long black stockings (to hide the scarred left leg), and with her limp and her long black braids, she was easy to spot on the campus. Even wearing the girls' uniform that her high school insisted upon—the white middy blouse and the mid-calf, dark-blue skirt—she stood out.

But Eileen was a quick study. In no time she had trimmed her hair and discarded the stockings. She made friends, and a few years later she co-hosted an elaborate tea party with one of them at a local hotel. The setting featured potted palms, and the entertainment included a harpist who played romantic airs from behind the palms. Eileen's mother assisted in receiving the guests, although she couldn't imagine why her daughter wanted to give a tea party, much less one that involved a harp.

When Eileen entered San Diego High, she was happy to discover that the school had an outstanding student newspaper, called *The Russ*. Eileen joined its staff as soon as she could and began contributing articles and poems. She had found her niche in high school, and she relished her status as a reporter.

In her senior year she was elected Editor-in-Chief of *The Russ*, the first girl ever to hold that position. Eileen always insisted that the student body voted for her out of sympathy. As she was crossing a street one night after a *Russ* meeting, an automobile went through a red light and struck her. She ended up in the hospital, with several broken bones. That, she said, was why she became editor of *The Russ*. The accident may have had something to do with her election, but the students who voted for her must have sensed that she could handle the job.

In those days *The Russ* staff received professional guidance and help from two local dailies, *The San Diego Sun*, which was a Scripps-Howard newspaper, and the *The San Diego Union*. *The Russ*'s editor was even allowed to borrow and use for publication engravings from the *Sun* when those engravings related to school activities. After the students elected Eileen editor of the *The Russ*, she met and became friends with some of the *Sun*'s editorial staff. Those contacts helped her land her first job on a major newspaper. In her senior year she not only edited her high-school paper, but she also worked after school as a cub reporter for the *Sun*.

*

Sometime during the spring of 1923, during her last semester of high school, Eileen agreed to go on a blind date. She wasn't sure she wanted to go—she disliked blind dates—but her girlfriend insisted that she would like the young Texas art student who was a friend of that girlfriend's boyfriend. The blind date began one spring evening, when the four drove to the beach together to attend a grunion hunt.

The young artist, who had recently left the Art Institute of Chicago and come to an art school in San Diego for his health's sake (he had developed strep throat in Chicago), was named Everett Jackson. He was twenty-two years old. Eileen had a powerful effect upon him that night. The two never left the car to look for grunion. They talked right through the grunion hunt. Everett was so overcome by Eileen that while they were still alone in the car he proposed to her. She told him that, flattered though she was, she was only seventeen and not about to marry anyone. After high school, she said, she was going to go to college, something neither of her parents had done, and she was going to write lots more newspaper articles. She agreed to go out with Everett again, however. They dated for several weeks, until he left for Mexico with a friend, to paint. From there he continued his courtship by mail.

*

The summer following Eileen's graduation from high school, she worked for the *Sun* full-time. After she started college in the fall at San Diego State (still known in 1923 as the Normal School), she went on working for the paper in her spare moments. She found it fairly easy to take classes and write for a newspaper, for in those days the college was situated close to her home and next to a streetcar line. After school she could jump on a streetcar and arrive downtown a short while later. Her career and studies would have been harder to juggle in 1931, when the campus was moved to its present site, ten miles east of town.

During Eileen's first year in college, she became a social columnist for the *Sun*, writing under the by-line "Señorita Diego." However, her interviews and feature stories carried her own name, Eileen Dwyer. Her newspaper clippings from those days reveal that she was given some impressive—and rare—assignments. Eileen says in her notes that "the Sun believed in giving its cub reporters challenging assignments, sometimes to its regret." At one point Eileen was asked to take over the "Cynthia Grey" column, in the absence of its regular columnist, who was on vacation. The "Cynthia Grey" column was the "Dear Abby" of that day. When a teenage reader asked advice on whether or not to kiss her beau good night at the end of a date, Eileen wrote, "Most assuredly, yes!" At that, the city editor pulled her from the column, judging her to be too immature for the job.

Apparently, however, the editor thought she was mature enough to interview the great ballerina Anna Pavlova, or at least he thought so at first. Pavlova had agreed to an interview, but when Eileen arrived at her hotel and presented herself, the little ballerina commented that Eileen seemed a bit young. In her notes describing that day, Eileen wrote:

> The Sun editor must have had misgivings about the success of the interview, since he sent his experienced reporter Max Miller to look in on the situation. The dancer mentioned my tender years to him. He told her this was my first interview, which I promptly denied, assuring her

> that it was my second. My first, I explained, had been with Edna Wallace Hopper, the ageless flapper. Pavlova was generous and gracious, giving me an affectionate kiss for encouragement at the end of the interview, and tickets to her performance that night.

While working on the *Sun*, Eileen also interviewed the opera singer Madame Ernestine Schumann-Heink. The famous contralto was then living in Coronado, California, just across the bay from San Diego. Eileen's editor knew that the singer was about to take a trip to New York, and he wanted to get an interview with her before she left. Eileen reported in her article:

> Madame Schumann-Heink interviewed herself, beginning: "I have eleven grandchildren. I'm sixty-four years old. I eat lots. All my teeth are my own, and I don't powder my nose. And now, Miss Reporter, what else do you want to know?"

The famous singer went on to say that she didn't like sob-sister stories, nor did she like sarcastic ones. Luckily she didn't know that Eileen could be a real sob sister when the occasion called for it.

*

Sometimes Eileen's assignments verged on the bizarre, and those were the ones that revealed her talent as a sob sister. One day Eileen's editor sent her off to interview the mother of a young San Diego man who had been executed at Folsom Prison. The son was said to have been an accomplice in the killing of a Los Angeles policeman. Eileen talked to the mother just before the young man's funeral took place, in a local Catholic church. The article that Eileen wrote afterwards was headed: "Mother Sobs Requiem At Boy Slayer's Bier." Eileen wrote:

> "They have crushed my boy to death." Little

> Mrs. George Montijo sobbed these words over and over today as she sat beside the coffin of her "baby," Edmond Montijo, 19-year-old boy who was hanged at Folsom Prison Friday.
>
> She combed a soft wave in his hair.
>
> And smiled.
>
> The little Irish mother had remained beside the body of the condemned boy since Sunday, when it arrived from Folsom …
>
> The boy was beautiful in death.
>
> His soft brown hair lay in loose waves on his high forehead, and on his thin face was a peculiar sweetness and restfulness, marked in contrast to the tear-stained face of his mother …

Reading that article, I am struck by just how mature Eileen's editor must have thought she was, to have sent her out on such an assignment, and I am relieved that eventually she became a full-time social columnist. That she possessed a talent for description is evident from the article above, but I am sure it's more pleasant to describe a woman's ball gown than the hair and facial expression of a young man in his coffin.

*

The pathos in Eileen's Montijo story must have impressed her editor, for soon he sent her off again on a human-interest assignment. This time she traveled to the San Diego county jail, to observe the visiting hour. The article she wrote afterwards had the following heading: "Babies 'Visits at Jail Bring Out Officers' Tenderness." Her article began:

> "Visiting hour-again." Herbert Kennedy, desk deputy sheriff at the county jail, sighed and continued pounding out reports on his typewriter.
>
> There is something sad and peculiarly fascinating about visiting hour at the San Diego county jail.

> The deputies always "stick around," because there is sure to be some tired little mother who is glad to turn baby over to them while she talks to "daddy."
>
> Visiting hour comes at noon, the most unromantic time of day, and yet the most unemotional person gulps a little when the visitors file in.

Eileen's editor gave her many opportunities to write such human-interest stories, and every now and then he allowed her to interview a famous person. But on one occasion she managed to get an interview which was not intended for her. Eileen wrote about this experience in her notes, saying:

> U.S. Senator Hiram W. Johnson, former Progressive Republican Governor of California and unsuccessful candidate for U.S. Vice President in 1912, was rumored to be en route here on his yacht. Senator Johnson was always "good copy" when he agreed to be interviewed. I was asked by the city editor to walk down to the waterfront to check the possible arrival of the yacht and to telephone him for further instructions.
>
> Assuming that I was being assigned to interview the Senator, if and when I did locate him, I asked the editor to give me a list of questions to ask the Senator. Perhaps to humor me and get me on the way, he suggested questions of such timely political significance that only a naive reporter would dare pose them and expect answers to them. The editor repeated, "*If* you find him, call in."
>
> I walked to the foot of Broadway only to learn that the yacht had arrived but gone on for refueling to what is now the area of the Destroyer Base.
>
> Losing no time I hopped on a streetcar and headed for the Destroyer Base area. Once there I ran down the long pier to the looming yacht and

jumped aboard. An amazed young man, who turned out to be a member of the Senator's family, questioned my unexpected invasion and intentions.

"I've come to interview the Senator," I announced boldly. The young man indicated I was being presumptuous to think the Senator would grant an interview.

Just then the Senator appeared on deck and seemed amused when I explained that I was there to get his views on some controversial national and international issues.

He asked to hear the questions, and obviously was intrigued by their probing nature. He agreed to the interview, providing I could guarantee that he would be quoted accurately. I agreed to read back his answers from my notes, which I did before being dismissed. I literally ran to the telephone booth at the end of the pier in order to relay my scoop to the editor before the first edition deadline.

To my surprise the editor was not elated with my success.

"Where in hell have you been, and why haven't you called in to the office?" he asked, revealing after I told him of my successful quest, that he had expected to send another reporter to do the interview. I got the point. I was the expendable cub, and had been used only as a messenger to track down the Senator.

It was too late now. He asked the experienced reporter he had in mind, Bert Andrews, to get the story from me—but fast!—over the telephone and to do the rewrite job. Bert couldn't believe my quotes, and warned me that they had better be accurate. He was amazed that the Senator would agree to answer such questions.

When I returned to the office from the pier telephone by slow streetcar, the first edition was on the street with the story streamlined but not by-lined. I learned it was also on the United Press wires.

Early in the afternoon W. H. Porterfield, who was at one time half-owner of the Sun with E. W. Scripps, arrived in the office, brandishing a rolled-up copy of the first edition. He boomed, "Who wrote this story?"

Bert pointed to me. I pointed to him. Porterfield loudly announced for the whole city-room staff to hear: "A bonus to both of you," and handed each of us $10.00. It was the only bonus for a scoop I ever received.

*

On October 6, 1924, Eileen covered her first wedding. It was a memorable one. As she wrote in her notes, "I was in the clouds at the first wedding I ever covered for the social press." The ceremony was performed in a little airplane three thousand feet over the city, and eighteen-year-old Eileen was riding in that plane as a witness. Her article began:

> "I—I do," came the voice of the little brunet bride over the roar of the airplane engine, which was at that particular moment 3,000 feet in the sky.
>
> With the heavens as the cathedral, and the engine hum for the music, Miss Mildred Ward became the bride of Glenn H. Brentner, with Judge Claude Chambers officiating, with Aviator A. A. Bennett and the writer as witnesses.
>
> Seven thousand wedding guests stood on the sands at Ocean Beach as the matrimonial plane soared high in the sky. The pre-honeymoon course took the bridal party across San Diego bay and along the waterfront. When the 3,000-foot altitude was reached, the pilot of the five-passenger ship … which is, incidentally, the largest plane of its kind

> in the state, signaled Judge Chambers to commence.

After the plane landed, the ceremony was repeated, with another judge officiating. No one could say for sure that the first ceremony was legal, so the bridal couple repeated their vows on the ground, just in case.

Eileen went on to cover literally thousands of weddings, over a long period of time. In fact, in 1990, she began to think she should retire for good (she had already tried it once) when an elderly couple asked her to write up their sixtieth wedding anniversary, and then reminded her that she had written up their wedding! But I'm sure that few of the weddings she subsequently covered were as thrilling and unique as that first one.

*

In 1925, during Eileen's sophomore year at San Diego State, she persuaded her editor at the *Sun* to let her become a reporter on the courthouse beat. She was the second woman in San Diego history to cover the court.

In her notes Eileen said that this advancement was to keep her from leaving the *Sun*. She had received an offer from *The San Diego Union* to become a social reporter on the *Union*, and the offer was such a good one she was seriously considering it. In her notes she wrote:

> I told the Sun editor that if I had to "do" society, a beat downgraded by most male staff members, I preferred to do it on the Union, which had a more society-oriented circulation. I added that I hoped someday to graduate to news coverage. Probably with some misgiving, he met the Union's proposed wage contract, and assigned me to general assignment and later to the Sun's coveted courthouse beat.

In 1925 there were only four Superior Court judges in San

Diego. Eileen liked all four of them, but her favorite was Judge William Paxton Cary. Judge Cary gave Eileen a scoop one day. He leaned across his desk and whispered to her, "I have an exclusive story for you!" He then announced the birth of his daughter, Margaret Virginia Cary. Years later Eileen and Judge Cary's wife, Jean, became good friends.

Eileen had a special relationship with a fifth judge, Judge Lloyd Griffin, who presided in Justice Court No. 1. Since her desk in the courthouse adjoined his office, she often served as a "bridesmaid" witness at the weddings he performed.

In June of 1925 Judge Griffin got into trouble. He committed a minor offense, if it could be called an offense at all, but it generated a great deal of comment. It also led to an amusing interview with Eileen.

A San Diego attorney criticized Judge Griffin for dancing too much. The attorney reported that on three consecutive days he had seen the judge dancing during the lunch hour at a local grill. The attorney said that he felt it was beneath the dignity of a judge to dance.

Feeling guilty, Judge Griffin gave up dancing for two weeks. But that was as long as he could stand still. In an interview with Eileen at the grill, he announced his decision.

"If it's a case of the justiceship or dancing," he said, "I choose the dance. I'd rather dance than do anything I know, and I don't care who knows it." Having said that, he asked his interviewer to join him in a dance.

Eileen reported in her notes that Judge Griffin's passion for dancing did not hurt his professional future. He later became presiding justice of the Fourth District Court of Appeal.

*

Eileen went on to write in her notes that "Judge Lacy Jennings, who presided over the criminal court, spoke out just as firmly on a less frivolous subject—the parole system." She quoted him as saying, "No individual who has committed an offense and broken his parole ever should be granted parole again."

In an interview with Judge Jennings, Eileen reported his views on the evils of the Jazz Age. In that interview he said:

> Jazz, gin and petting parties … there's the modern triangle at whose feet you can throw the crime wave. Broad-mindedness—pooh! What we need is more simplicity of life … We've got to fight modernism … it's the age that's at fault.

Eileen was a conscientious courthouse reporter, who prided herself on her accuracy. She always made an effort to get her facts straight. But because she was also a reporter who cared about people, she couldn't resist injecting human interest into her stories. During a lengthy bribery trial that involved a city councilman, she described the defendant's daughter-in-law and the daughter-in-law of the plaintiff as they sat next to each other in the courtroom:

> Sitting side by side, their beauty in direct contrast … one a colorful brunet, the other a radiant blonde … estranged before they had a chance to be friends … [they] watched with minute interest their first court trial.

In other articles about that case, Eileen described the defendant's wife as "white-haired and sweet," and she wrote that the presiding judge was "a regular fellow … the kind of fellow who smokes fragrant cigars and puffs them chummily."

Eileen always looked for the human interest in a story. She could no more edit that part out of her writing than Judge Griffin could stop dancing.

Two articles Eileen wrote in 1925 told a very human story. A San Diego woman became a news item when a Superior Court jury found her guilty of grand larceny. Eileen's first article dealt with the woman's reaction to her court experience. Stung by the Deputy District Attorney's description of her as "an abcess in the flesh of San Diego," and no doubt depressed by her conviction, she took poison (obtained from a girlfriend who was attending the trial) and landed in the emergency room of a local hospital.

She survived, and a short while later Eileen wrote her up again. It seems that by then the matron of the San Diego County jail had appointed this convicted larcenist to be the "housekeeper" of the jail. The woman, now recovered from her suicide attempt, had turned into a veritable "Slave Driver." She was cleaning up the place, and was forcing the other women prisoners to dust, sweep, and mop. Their quarters had never looked so clean. The other women were muttering mutinously, but so far the "Slave Driver" was totally in command.

*

Eileen was gaining experience every day as she covered the courthouse beat, and she was meeting some interesting people. They were not all convicted larcenists. The newlyweds whose weddings she witnessed in Judge Griffin's chambers often sent her boxes of candy, to thank her for her services. Now one of those boxes led her to a famous poet.

In those days the city room of the *Sun* was open to visiting reporters who might want to use the *Sun*'s typewriters when passing through the city. One day a stranger came into the city room to use a typewriter, and he chose an empty desk next to the one where Eileen was sitting. Eileen offered him some of her chocolates, which he accepted with a smile. The next day he appeared again, and again accepted some of her candy. The city editor, who was positioned at the other end of the room, telephoned Eileen to ask her who that man was who was eating her chocolates.

Eileen asked the man his name, and when he replied, "Carl Sandburg," she telephoned the information to the city editor. The name sounded familiar to her, and it greatly excited the editor. He had heard a rumor that the famous poet and newsman Carl Sandburg was in town. The editor asked Eileen to invite Mr. Sandburg to have tea later in the day with some of the members of the staff. Mr. Sandburg accepted the invitation. The editor also invited Eileen to join the group, since by then it was clear that she had become Mr. Sandburg's friend.

As Eileen talked to the poet over tea, she remembered why his name had sounded so familiar. His poems were in an anthology of poetry that had been her required text in a college English class. And one of his poems was on a test she had taken.

"Oh, I know what you wrote!" she said. "You wrote 'Mending Wall.'"

"No," Mr. Sandburg said, "that was Robert Frost."

"Then I guess you wrote ..." and Eileen named another poem that Mr. Sandburg had not written.

Again he shook his head.

"Well," said Eileen, "there was only one more poem that was on that test, so you must have written 'Grass.'"

Mr. Sandburg smiled and confirmed her statement that "Grass" was a poem he had written.

*

Eileen was happy to be covering the courthouse beat. She liked the way her career was progressing. But her personal life bothered her. She wanted to see that artist again.

Marriage

By the spring of 1925 Eileen and the young artist in Mexico had corresponded with each other for almost two years. Eileen was beginning to fall in love with him through the mail. When he suggested that they meet again in person, she responded favorably. She had had in mind transferring to the University of Arizona for her third year of college, and Everett told her that he thought that was an excellent idea. In those days, when people traveled by train, not plane, it would be easier for Everett to reach Tucson, Arizona, from Mexico than to reach the far western city of San Diego.

Eileen was eager to leave San Diego for a while. Attending classes at a campus a few miles from her house was all right, but it reminded her of high school. She was ready for a new collegiate experience. She wanted to "go away to college."

Her grades were good, so she had no trouble transferring. Once she was established on the Arizona campus, she began writing articles for the college paper. Before long she had pledged a sorority, Gamma Phi Beta. She felt like a real coed at last.

After she was initiated into the Gamma Phi sorority, one of her sorority sisters told her that during rushing some members of the group had expressed concern that she might leave college after only a few months "to marry that artist she was always writing to." An advisor to the sorority—an older, tart-tongued Gamma Phi from back East—had said, "Pledge her! It doesn't matter if she doesn't stay long. She'll bring more credit to our sorority than any other girl I know."

That winter Everett came up from Mexico to visit Eileen. By the time the visit was over, they had reached an understanding.

They made plans to marry the following summer.

*

During the two years when Eileen was working on the *Sun* and attending San Diego State, she dated a number of young men. She went out with several college students, but she preferred the company of newspapermen. One newsman, a fellow reporter, almost persuaded her to marry him. The man's name was Sam Jackson, which might lead one to suspect that Eileen Dwyer was fated to become Eileen Jackson someday.

Sam was older than the college boys Eileen dated, a good ten years older. He was tough and experienced, the kind of reporter Eileen admired. Perhaps he was too experienced, her mother thought. My grandmother was rooting for Everett.

Sam Jackson fell in love with Eileen and asked her to marry him. She was torn, for Sam was not only an appealing man, but he was also someone from her world. He understood the journalists' world of by-lines, deadlines, and adrenaline rushes.

After Everett visited her in Arizona, though, Eileen knew that he was the man she wanted to marry. When she returned home, she told Sam this. He took it well, wished her a lifetime of happiness, and a few months later moved from San Diego, to work for a newspaper in another city.

Eileen never saw Sam Jackson again. Forty years later, however, in the 1960s, two of Eileen's friends—a mother and daughter—attended a conference in Sacramento. At the conference they met and spoke with an attractive older man in his late sixties or early seventies. Hearing that they were from San Diego, he asked them if, by any chance, they knew a woman there named Eileen Dwyer Jackson. Eileen's two friends informed the man that they often saw Eileen and that she was a good friend of theirs.

"I used to date her, back in the twenties," the man said. "We worked on a paper together. How is she, and how does she look?"

"She's fine, and she looks beautiful," one of the women told him.

"She still looks very young," the other said. "She probably

looks just about the way she did when you knew her."

"Please give her a message from me," said the man. "Tell her Sam Jackson says hello, and tell her that I'll love her till I die."

Eileen's friends gave her that message when they returned home. Eileen did not share the message with Everett, but she did repeat it to me. Of course I am very glad that my mother chose Everett Jackson over Sam, but I can't forget Sam's words. What woman wouldn't feel pleased and touched to receive a message like that after forty years?

*

Eileen and Everett were married July 21, 1926, in El Paso, Texas. They had chosen El Paso because it was halfway between San Diego and Everett's East Texas hometown. Also, it was close to Mexico, where they were to honeymoon.

Eileen's parents and brother were unable to attend the wedding. My grandmother was ill, and even Christian Science couldn't cure her in time to make the long train trip to Texas. Eileen's father, a dear, shy man who had not yet met the bridegroom (my grandfather had never come out into the living room when Everett was dating Eileen in 1923), remained in San Diego to care for my grandmother, so Eileen came to Texas by herself. Until the wedding, she stayed at the home of her maid of honor, a sorority sister who lived in El Paso.

Eileen and Everett had originally scheduled the wedding for July 19, but several days before that date Everett developed a high fever. After some discussion, he and Eileen agreed to postpone the ceremony. Most of the large Jackson clan on hand for the festivities fled to the mountains to escape the heat. They planned to return the following week, when the rescheduled wedding would take place.

On July 21, while most of his relatives were still in the mountains, Everett insisted he felt well enough to marry. In the presence of his parents, one brother, who served as his best man, and Eileen's maid of honor, Eileen and Everett were married. The *El Paso Times* reported that "the bride was costumed in white crepe de chine, with matching accessories, and scarf and picture hat of orchid. The maid of honor wore a frock of blonde georgette, with matching hat and accessories." I have no idea who gave my mother away. Probably she gave herself.

By the time the other Jackson relatives returned from the mountains, the newlyweds were on a train headed deep into Mexico. They were on their way to Lake Chapala, in the state of Jalisco. Eileen's life with Everett had begun.

*

One week later the two moved into their first home. It was a beautiful old lakeshore villa just outside the little town of Chapala. The house, which was called El Manglar, had originally belonged to the brother of President Porfirio Díaz. Everett had rented it the month before his wedding, and had hired a family of servants to take care of it and to cook for him and Eileen. Since the house was so large, my father's recent companions in Mexico, the artist Lowell Houser and a young Texas chum named Traynham Pitts, were able to fit easily into one of the wings. They had been living with Everett in the village of Ajijic before his marriage, and they were delighted when Everett's new bride invited them to move into El Manglar. Eileen, the former career woman, was now Eileen, the hospitable chatelaine of a crumbling but romantic old mansion.

She took to her new life the way she had taken to writing for a newspaper. She read books, accompanied Everett on his painting expeditions into the hills above the lake, swam in mountain pools with him, and presided over the candlelit dinner table at night like a queen in her castle.

Lowell and Traynham dined with the honeymooners each noon and night but otherwise tried to stay out of their way. Occasionally the four would travel together to a nearby village, and the outing was always an enjoyable experience.

In later years Eileen often described her honeymoon as "a year of constant laughter." In a letter she wrote to her parents from Chapala, she said, "I laugh so much these days that I should find it hard to cry again ... Each day becomes more golden."

She told her parents about a ceremony she and the other three took part in that made them all laugh:

> We are nuts! You would marvel at the crazy things we do. At noon during our long meal we set a clay idol in a silver dish with green-yellow lemons at its feet and place the dish in the center of the table. We place an avocado in the clay basket on the back of the mono or idol, and a smoking cigarette in its mouth. That is during dinner. After dinner we fill the clay basket with tequila, and set fire to the tequila. It gives a weird blue, poisonous flame. Then we all kneel on the floor, put our heads bowed, with eyes shut, on the table and pray.
>
> Traynham prays aloud to the idol, who is our "income idol." We all pray for an income. Traynham prays in his preacher's voice: "Income idol, please make the income come in."
>
> That is an example of what nuts we are.

Eileen also wrote her parents that she and Everett planned to wait eight years before having a child "as we have a great deal to do—work and traveling. It would be nice then I think and we could take it with us and let its life be interesting."

Eileen and Everett had plans to go to Spain the following year, and then to Italy. They had many lovely plans. But I was born two years later—not eight—and then came the Depression and World War II. Eileen and Everett finally reached Spain in 1965, and Italy in 1969.

*

In October the Chapala foursome moved on to Mexico City. Eileen and Everett rented a house in the suburb of Coyoacán and found two servants to take care of them. Their idyll continued, and they began to meet some fascinating people—the painters Jean Charlot and José Clemente Orozco, the writer Anita Brenner, and others. A Chicago Art Institute classmate of

Everett and Lowell's, a watercolorist named Jules Billington, joined them for a while.

In a letter to her parents, Eileen reported that she and Everett did not want to become part of the "studio crowd" in Mexico City. She said that Anita Brenner, whom they knew through Lowell, had invited them to a "celebrity party," where they were to meet Diego Rivera. She explained that they had already gone to a few smaller parties involving members of that crowd and had found the group too sophisticated for their tastes. Eileen told her parents that the people at those parties "all drank and smoked and said pretty, clever, wild and naughty things." She wrote:

> I don't think we will go … if we accept too many invitations we will get into an unhappy, expensive social routine … It is easy to have friends here.
>
> Already we are further in a group than we care to be and it is the most celebrated group on this hemisphere we are made to understand …

As a result of their scruples Eileen and Everett never met Diego Rivera. However, they liked the two artists they did meet that fall—Orozco and Jean Charlot. Charlot became a good friend and later visited them in San Diego. But my parents decided to avoid the Bohemian parties of Mexico City, even though famous artists were always present at those affairs.

Perhaps they regretted that decision later, but I doubt it. Eileen and Everett never sought out celebrities. They would meet many over the years because of their work, but they never went looking for famous people.

In December of 1926 Traynham returned to the United States, and Lowell, who had taken a job with the Carnegie Institution, left for the ruins of Yucatán. Eileen and Everett spent a happy Christmas together—just the two of them—in Mexico City. Shortly after that, Eileen started writing again.

Of course she had never really stopped. For five months she had poured her creative energy into letter-writing. Her letters to her parents were filled with amusing anecdotes and beautiful descriptive passages. Now, however, as 1927 approached, she felt it was time to produce some articles as well as letters. First she wrote a story for *The San Diego Sun* about the threatening political situation in Mexico. Then she wrote an article on the "Mexican Modern Movement" and submitted it, under her maiden name, to the London art magazine *The Studio*. *The Studio* accepted her article and published it in October of 1927. Eileen illustrated it with photographs of murals by Orozco, Diego Rivera, and Robert Montenegro, and with a photo of a large painting by Everett entitled "Mexican Jungle."

Eileen was no dummy. By writing as Eileen Dwyer, she was able to call attention to Everett and to praise him. Because of her last name, her readers would assume that she was a detached observer, not his doting wife. In the article she said:

> Mexico City more than ever is now a hive of young modernists who come to escape the impressionists of the United States and Europe, and whose crying desire is to understand and portray—form, design and colour.
>
> The most interesting of the American group, perhaps, is Everett Gee Jackson. The mass, not the line plane, interests him. Before other elements his work has this "weight" dimension ... It is the richness of Jackson's colour and his "turning volumes" that are most noteworthy.

Eileen also got in a nice plug for Lowell:

> Houser, who works in tempera almost altogether, concerns himself especially with design. He is now on the artists' staff of the Carnegie expedition, which is excavating for Maya art in Yucatán.

Eileen was pleased with herself. At age twenty, with just a

little help from Everett on artistic terminology, she had had an article accepted by a respected London publication.

*

That January Eileen and Everett moved south, to the town of Tehuantepec. Again they found a house and settled down. Everett painted some of his most powerful paintings while he and Eileen were living in southern Mexico. They both looked forward to spending many months in Tehuantepec, but they had to adjust their thinking when Everett became ill with malaria. After he recovered, his doctor advised him to leave the tropics. The honeymooners slowly made their way north. It was time for them to go home.

Everett's mother had paid for this magical honeymoon, with money from her oil well. Some years before, she had inherited a small piece of land in Texas. When an oil company expressed an interest in drilling a well on her land, she said, "Drill away," but she refused to sell her mineral rights. Everett's father pointed out to her that all the wells the companies were drilling in that area were coming in "dry." He urged her to sell the mineral rights and take the sizable amount of cash that the oil company was offering. She decided to gamble instead, a wise move, for her well did not come in "dry." It turned out to be one of the biggest gushers in Texas.

My Texas grandmother had a wonderful time with her money. She showered it on her seven children and their families. She had never had much spending money before; my grandfather had always given her just enough to run the house. But now she was able to send children to college, to buy cars and homes for them, and to subsidize my father while he painted for four years in Mexico, one of which years was his honeymoon.

Upon their return to the United States, Eileen and Everett moved into a little house called the Hunter's Den (or the Den, for short), which was situated on some land Everett's family owned near Palestine, Texas. In that unspoiled wilderness—nearly four hundred acres of trees, shrubs, and cold, clear springs—the two enjoyed a peaceful fall. Then, in December, Eileen discovered she was pregnant.

*

I was born in San Diego, California, in August of 1928. My Jackson grandfather had hoped I would be born at the Den, but my mother wanted to be near her own mother for such an important event.

At the time of my birth Eileen and Everett were staying with Eileen's parents. It was supposed to be a short-term arrangement, but because of the Depression the two families ended up living together for the next seven years. In 1928 and 1929 it was the younger couple who needed a refuge, but from 1930 to 1935 it was the older. During the Depression years building ceased in San Diego, and contractors found themselves out of work.

Everett took his new responsibilities seriously. He appreciated the allowance he received from his mother, but his aim was to do without it. Since there were no Mexican idols in San Diego to pray to for income, and since he only sold a painting every now and then, he knew he would have to find a real job, the kind that paid a salary.

First, however, he enrolled at San Diego State. He already had credits from Texas A&M, the school he had attended before the Art Institute, and in June of 1930 he obtained his bachelor's degree. In 1929, before he completed his studies at State, he taught for a summer at Sul Ross College in West Texas. He had considered getting his degree from Sul Ross and staying on there to teach, but I became ill in Texas and Eileen grew homesick, so the three of us returned to California. In November of 1930 a position in the art department opened at San Diego State, and Everett got the job.

For sixteen months after my birth Eileen tried to be a housewife. With her tremendous energy she threw herself into motherhood and housework. In the fall of 1928 she received an offer from one of the San Diego papers to become a reporter again, but Everett said that wives were not supposed to work outside the home. He was quite definite about that.

In 1928 and 1929, however, Eileen did do some freelance writing. During that time she had three articles published, one in the London quarterly *Artwork*, and two in the San Francisco art journal *The Argus*. Her article in *Artwork* was about Everett. Her two in *The Argus* were about the artists of Mexico and about the San Diego painter Charles Reiffel.

Eileen waited three years before submitting another article to a magazine, but when she did, it was not only accepted but awarded a prize. In November of 1932 her story entitled "An Old San Diego Home is Rejuvenated" was published in *Sunset* and won first prize in that magazine's "Home Improvement Contest."

*

During that period in the late twenties when Eileen was a housewife, she made two friends whom she would know and enjoy for years afterwards. One was a Gamma Phi from Oregon, a tiny, energetic woman named Bea Evenson. Eileen and Bea met at a Gamma Phi alumni meeting, and they liked each other right away.

At that point in her life, Bea considered herself a homemaker. Years later, however, after her children were grown, she would become a dynamic civic leader. In 1965 she spearheaded a successful drive to develop a landscaped park along a portion of San Diego's waterfront. It is now known as Spanish Landing. She then crusaded (also successfully) to preserve the Spanish Colonial architecture in San Diego's Balboa Park.

Eileen was always drawn to lively women like herself. Those two housewives, meeting at a sorority alumni party, didn't know that they were both destined to make a mark on San Diego someday. But they did know that they wanted to see more of each other. Over the years Bea and her husband, Frank, often camped with my parents. Bea was a civic powerhouse in town, and a cheery, enthusiastic camper in the country.

The other woman Eileen met and took to in the 1920s was also a vivacious, energetic person. Her name was Myrle Murray.

She was a well-off woman—another housewife—who had had a baby girl just one month before Eileen had me. They met through my grandfather, who was doing some building for the Murrays. Some years after Myrle's first husband died, she married a man named Ray Cavell. Like Bea Evenson and Eileen, Myrle thought there was more to life than puttering around a house. In her mid-years she took up real estate, formed her own company, and became one of San Diego's most successful career women. She and Eileen remained close friends for sixty-seven years.

Eileen was glad to have found new friends during her housewife period, but toward the end of 1929 she was beginning to act a little squirrelly. Her mother was cooking the meals and devoting a great deal of time to me. Eileen didn't have enough to do, so she started making up things to do. She had too much energy, and she missed being a reporter.

Often that fall Everett would come home from his afternoon college classes and find her on her knees scrubbing the kitchen floor. "But one day," he said, with his grand Texas hyperbole, "I came home and found she'd taken up the linoleum from the kitchen floor, and was scrubbing *under* the linoleum, so I told her if she was going to work *that* hard, she might as well make some money!"

On January 1, 1930, Eileen joined the staff at *The San Diego Union* as the *Union*'s society editor. In May of that year she began writing a social column called "Tete-a-Tete." It was the first of its kind in San Diego.

Social Reporting During the Depression

Eileen would have preferred the courthouse beat again, but she was happy to have a job at all in 1930. The stock market had crashed on October 29, 1929, and by the winter of 1930 San Diegans were beginning to realize that they were facing a serious depression. It had not sunk in right away. Now, however, a few months after the stock-market crash, people were starting to lose their jobs, bankruptcies were occurring, and few employers were hiring.

Eileen knew that her days of covering the courthouse beat were over. The *Union* would never give that assignment to a woman during the Depression, when men were so in need of work. Luckily for Eileen, the editor who hired her believed that women were better qualified than men to cover social events, and he was determined to keep the social coverage going.

Sometime later, in the mid-1930s, a male employee at the paper snapped at Eileen, "You shouldn't be working here. You're taking the job some man should have."

Eileen softly reminded him that she put out a Women's Page, that, although men's names appeared in her copy, she mostly wrote for and about women. "Few male reporters," she said, "want to write about women." The man admitted that was true.

Social life did go on in San Diego during the Depression. People continued to attend weddings and parties, to do club work, to take trips. Admittedly, the parties were nowhere near as frequent or as lavish as the ones that would be given after World War II, and during the thirties fewer people traveled abroad. But social activity existed, and Eileen knew it. Her first task after she went back to work in 1930 was to find out who was doing what in San Diego County, and who was going where.

Her second task was to think up some gimmicks to entice her readers. She felt that if a newspaper wanted to encourage the readership of women during the Depression, that paper would have to provide cheerful, entertaining articles in the society section to counteract the front-page news. The national news was gloomy and discouraging in those days, but Eileen saw no reason for the social pages to reflect the downcast state of the nation. Her fertile mind quickly came up with some ideas to attract women readers to the paper.

By August of 1930 she had begun a weekly series of articles entitled "Hobbies That Bring Happiness." Each week she featured a different San Diego matron and described that woman's hobby. A photo of the woman, holding or demonstrating some aspect of her hobby, always accompanied the article.

Most of the hobbies were predictable: gardening, painting, collecting. One woman did say that the school she had founded was her hobby, and several women considered their hobbies to be their volunteer work. But most described, and were pictured with, their collections. The women tended to collect such objects as dolls, antiques, snuff bottles, and shawls. A few of the collectors favored first editions, and some collected drawings and prints. One woman, Mrs. Irving Snyder of Coronado, managed to collect snuff boxes, stamps, first editions, *and* prints. She once loaned her collection of prints—by Rembrandt, Delacroix, Marie Laurencin, and others—to San Diego's art museum for an exhibit. As a collector, Mrs. Snyder surely took the prize.

The "Hobbies That Bring Happiness" feature continued for over a year. Then, on December 13, 1931, Eileen began a series of articles on the old mansions of San Diego, a series called "The Romances of Old San Diego Homes."

In the early thirties she also began writing short weekly editorials—she called them "social editorials"—on a variety of subjects. To her surprise, men as well as women enjoyed reading them. She let her imagination soar when writing those little essays; she wrote about anything that came to mind.

Sometimes her editorials contained information about the latest social trends (brides signing up with bridal registries, for instance, a new development in the thirties). Sometimes the editorials offered advice on etiquette. Some were witty and others poignant, but all were immensely readable.

Her public responded with enthusiasm. Most of the fan letters Eileen received over the years mentioned her editorials. People referred to them as "little gems," and those same people expressed amazement that she could come up with a different topic every week.

Eileen hoped the women of San Diego would like her innovations, and would therefore keep on subscribing to the *Union*. But the feature articles and the editorials were not the only enticements. Each day Eileen's column, "Tete-a-Tete," overflowed with social news. Just as she had found such news in her district of Ramona, where it was not supposed to exist, she now found it in Depression-ridden San Diego.

The items in her August 30, 1931, column reveal that San Diegans owned yachts and vacation houses at the beach; they gave supper parties and dances; that summer they had taken trips to England, Germany, even Russia; they had also traveled to distant parts of the United States. In her column Eileen admitted that "our San Diegans-abroad colony is unusually small this season." Still, the fact that people went abroad at all is of interest. Obviously, not everyone was hurting during the Depression.

Some people were publicity-shy, however. Some women turned Eileen down when she called them for news. Those women explained that their husbands did not want social publicity when they were letting employees go. Other women were happy to be written up, but they had a favor to ask. Back then almost every woman who attended the annual Charity Ball would beg Eileen, "When you describe my ball gown, please make it sound *old*! I don't want anyone to think I've bought a new dress!" In later decades Eileen would often describe old ball gowns and, to the delight of the owners, make the gowns sound new. During the thirties, however—in those "days of readjustment," as she referred to the Depression in print—she was supposed to stress how ancient the dresses were.

The Depression was a reality, even though one might not

think so when reading Eileen's column. Eventually, even the Charity Ball became a Depression casualty. It was canceled in 1935, and did not appear again until after the war.

Eileen's column, "Tete-a-Tete," served the same purpose as many of the movies of that day. She wrote about a world where glamorous people danced, gave parties, and had fun. The average housewife, who was struggling along without much money, could escape into that glamorous world for as long as it took to read the social page.

As Eileen became more involved with social reporting, she discovered that she liked it. The fact was, she liked people. She liked them whether they were society types or women like little Mrs. Montijo, the mother of that executed boy. As long as Eileen could talk to people, and write about them, she was happy. She would have preferred the courthouse beat, and she would always look back with pride on her days as a courthouse reporter, but she took her assignments as they came. She was too dedicated a reporter to moan and whine about "what might have been." She threw herself into her work as though all her life she had wanted to write up nothing but yachting parties and benefit balls.

*

In the 1930s Eileen wrote up more parties than she attended. The days when she would go to one almost every night were far off in the future. During the Depression she obtained most of her news over the phone. In the evening she was more likely to be home typing an editorial than out at a party. But although her job did not require her to go out every night, she and Everett did attend parties during those years. Some were more interesting than others. Once in a while an internationally known figure would appear in town. Then someone would give a party for that person. The honored guest would usually add a special sparkle to the event. One man, in particular, did his part to enliven such a gathering.

On November 17, 1931, a San Diego couple gave a small reception in their home in honor of the English philosopher and author Bertrand Russell. Included among the guests were Eileen and Everett. Earlier that evening Mr. Russell had participated in a debate on the subject of marriage and morals. Many people considered his views extreme, so Eileen was eager to meet him. She and Everett had brought a bottle of fine Scotch whiskey to the party, a gift to them from one of Eileen's favorite socialite friends, Mrs. Claus Spreckels of Coronado. As the Eighteenth Amendment had not yet been repealed, Mr. Russell was delighted to see that whiskey.

The combination of the Scotch and Eileen's beauty must have intoxicated him. Perhaps the subject of the debate that evening had had an effect. At any rate, my father told me that Bertrand Russell chased Eileen all around the kitchen that night in an attempt to kiss her. He told her she was gorgeous. Unable to achieve his goal, he finally settled on autographing a copy of his book *The Scientific Outlook* for my parents, and giving them a signed photograph of himself. Eileen decided that night that although she wasn't sure about his views, his actions certainly were extreme.

*

Two of Eileen's columns had more to say on the subject of the Eighteenth Amendment. In 1932 Franklin D. Roosevelt was elected President of the United States on a platform that promised the repeal of Prohibition. On December 11, 1932, Eileen wrote:

> Will teas become cocktail parties by Christmas, or rather, will they become cocktail parties in print by Christmas? As a matter of fact lots of them are already cocktail parties, but in print, as far as local publications are concerned, they are still charmingly appointed teas.

A year later, of course, the matter was settled. On December 17, 1933, Eileen stated in her column:

> Christmas comes to cheer up a red-letter Blue

> Monday this year and its cheer is the most legitimate and honest we've had in 13 years. Eggnog parties will not be teas, and Tom and Jerrys will be Tom and Jerrys in and out of print. There'll be real spirit in the mince pie and irreproachable brandy burnt on the plum pudding.

*

During her long career, Eileen interviewed the wives of eight United States Presidents. On June 21, 1933, she met the first of those wives, Mrs. Herbert Hoover. At that time Herbert Hoover was the nation's only living ex-President.

The Hoovers had driven south from Los Angeles that day to have lunch with their old friend Colonel Ira Copley and his wife, in the Copleys' Coronado home. Colonel Copley owned the *Union*, which was why Eileen was able to get the interview.

While the Hoovers were lunching in the dining room, Eileen sat on the veranda of the house, along with Henry Love, a political reporter from the *Union*, and Harry Bishop, a *Union* photographer. As the three waited together, they began to speculate on the former President's mood. They wondered how he was feeling now that he had lost the election and was no longer President. Eileen described that June day in one of her journals:

> Immediately after luncheon, Colonel Copley and the recent President arrived on the veranda where Henry Love was to interview Mr. Hoover. I sat in on the first, and more dramatic, phase of that interview, before joining Mrs. Hoover on an assignment of my own.
>
> "Make them human," Colonel Copley whispered to us as we started our challenging assignment.
>
> At first Herbert Hoover seemed in good humor, even when he announced that politics were out as a subject of conversation.
>
> He said he was enjoying what he called his first

real holiday since he had started to earn his living years before.

I commented to Mr. Hoover on his rested appearance, adding that he looked years younger in person than in photographs taken during the difficult days of his administration. It was suggested that Mrs. Hoover's well-known concern for his health and happiness and his first real vacation had helped to erase the tired lines.

"No," he replied, adding with the hint of a smile, "it was the Democrats!"

That was the nearest any of us got to politics, I observed in my story the next day.

President Hoover then sat down on a veranda rattan chair. He seemed so relaxed and amiable that the photographer, Harry Bishop, tried to sneak a candid photograph, which he hoped would reveal the real Hoover.

This seemed to disconcert Mr. Hoover. He stood up so abruptly he knocked the porch chair backward and nearly fell himself. Alarmed, we all reached to steady him. He indicated that Mr. Bishop's effort to get an unposed photograph had brought Love's interview to an end before it ever got started.

Colonel Copley smoothly intervened, calmed his annoyed distinguished friend, and arranged for the interview to continue. Hoover then agreed to pose for a conventional photograph which depicted him unsmiling and stern in the Union the next day.

After things had calmed down on the veranda, I joined Mrs. Hoover. I was well aware of Mrs. Hoover's attitude about interviews … She made a point of not giving them …

She made the situation easy for me, her eyes smiling beneath heavy dark brows as she said, "Shall we call it a stroll in a garden—not an interview?"

We walked together down the cool shaded paths that threaded through the colorful Copley garden.

I noted in my garden-stroll story that Mrs. Hoover had ready humor, unreserved laughter and a sweet grace—a graciousness which did not seem cultivated to be worn as an armor against first meetings.

*

Perhaps the most glamorous woman whose name appeared in Eileen's column during the thirties was Mrs. Claus Spreckels of Coronado. Her father-in-law, John D. Spreckels, of the Spreckels sugar fortune, had once owned *The San Diego Union* and the Coronado Hotel. Ellis Moon Spreckels was a beautiful blonde socialite, a woman of great wealth who sailed through the Depression years as though she were still living back in the carefree 1920s. In the thirties she often traveled to Europe, and she had a butler, a chauffeur, and a governess for her children. She lived in a large ocean-front house, which I visited on several occasions as a child.

When Eileen and Mrs. Spreckels first met, they discovered that they each had a two-year-old daughter. Mrs. Spreckels was older than Eileen—her little girl had been an "afterthought" baby—but in spite of their age difference and the difference in their backgrounds, they began what turned out to be a close, enduring friendship.

Ellis Spreckels was a cultivated woman, well read and seriously interested in art. She told Eileen that she wanted to enlarge her circle to include some local artists and writers. One night she gave a small dinner party in her home for Eileen and Everett and some of their artistic friends. Included at the party were the ornithologist and writer Griffing Bancroft and the newly famous author Max Miller.

Eileen always giggled when she described that party. She said she was amazed that Ellis still wanted to know any artists and writers after that night.

During the main course of the dinner, Griffing Bancroft dug

into his squab and sent it flying off his plate. As it fell to the floor, Everett cried, "Watch out for the dog!"

Max Miller shouted, "Don't worry; I've got my foot on it!" Eileen said that at that point even the dignified butler started to smile. Then, when the flaming dessert arrived, the tablecloth somehow caught on fire. No one's fault really, but still ...

Mrs. Spreckels was a good sport. At the end of the evening she told her guests that she hoped they would all come back and dine with her again.

In 1936, after the death of her first husband, Ellis married a prominent surgeon, Dr. E. Clarence Moore, of Los Angeles. From then on she spent most of her time in that city, although she did keep her Coronado house for occasional use. Eileen missed Ellis after she moved away, but was glad that Ellis had found happiness in her second marriage.

In 1935, when the world's attention was focused on the romantic drama taking place in England, Ellis Spreckels had firsthand knowledge of the couple involved. Fifteen years before, she had known both the Prince of Wales and his American friend, Mrs. Ernest Simpson. But in 1920 Wallis Simpson had been Mrs. Winfield Spencer, a resident of Coronado and the wife of a lieutenant commander in the United States Navy. In April of 1920 Ellis Spreckels had entertained the Prince of Wales and his cousin Louis Mountbatten in her Coronado home. The Prince was making a goodwill journey around the world, and San Diego was one of his stops. Fifteen years later, in 1935, Ellis visited Wallis in London at the height of Mrs. Simpson's romance with the Prince. When Ellis got home, she described the visit to Eileen.

My mother found all of this fascinating. I knew nothing of princes and their affairs. I only knew that Mrs. Spreckels always looked beautiful, and that she was warm and loving toward me whenever I spent the night with her quiet, gentle daughter, Claire.

Eileen enjoyed hearing about Wallis in 1935, and in the years that followed she continued to take an interest in that adventurous lady. She never got to meet the Duchess of Windsor, but the Duchess always intrigued her.

Eileen knew another woman who had known Wallis when she was living in Coronado. Mrs. Irving Snyder, the hobbyist whose collection of prints had rated an exhibit in the San Diego art museum, had also been a friend of Wallis Spencer's back in the early twenties. When the Spencers moved from the San Diego area, Mrs. Snyder and Wallis began a correspondence, which they kept up for several years.

Many years after the King had abdicated to marry Wallis Simpson, Mrs. Snyder invited Eileen and Everett to her home. Sitting in front of her fireplace, facing a blazing fire, she read them a number of letters written by Wallis when Wallis was still Wallis Spencer and when her marriage to Commander Spencer was collapsing. After reading the letters, Mrs. Snyder threw them into the fire. She said she didn't want those "confessional" letters to be "scrutinized by posterity." Eileen was shocked. She felt she had just witnessed the destruction of a small but valuable footnote to history.

*

San Diegans followed Mrs. Simpson's romance with interest, but in 1935 and 1936 the California-Pacific International Exposition provided them with additional entertainment. The exposition, which was held in San Diego's spacious Balboa Park, attracted many out-of-town visitors. Its two most distinguished visitors were President and Mrs. Franklin D. Roosevelt. They arrived in San Diego on October 1, 1935, and were taken to the Coronado Hotel. That evening Eileen met her second United States President and her second First Lady.

Eileen was one of the reporters assigned to cover the reception at the hotel honoring the President and his wife. Although she was happy to cover the reception, what she wanted to do most of all was to interview Mrs. Roosevelt the next day. She thought that if she could meet Mrs. Roosevelt before the rest of the press did, the First Lady might grant her an interview.

Eileen enlisted the aid of a friend, a woman who was a member of the official greeting party and the wife of one of San Diego's civic leaders. The friend thought it would be fun to help

Eileen. "I'll get you into the reception ahead of the press," she said. "We'll go in together. You can pretend to be my daughter!"

It worked for a minute. Eileen swept into the presidential suite on the arm of her "mother" and got well into the room. She was approaching the President when the Secret Service men caught up with her. They had figured out that her name wasn't on the guest list; it was on the press list. They were pretty sure that she wasn't the daughter of anyone in that room. They apprehended her and told her that she had to leave and go in later with the press.

President Roosevelt became aware that something was going on. When he asked what was happening, the Secret Service men informed him that Eileen didn't belong there. They explained that she was a member of the press, and that they were about to lead her away.

President Roosevelt looked at Eileen and gave her the warmest, most radiant smile she had ever seen. She often told people later that his smile seemed to say, "Where have you been all my life!"

"She doesn't look as though she could hurt anybody," the President said, and he indicated that Eileen was to stay. Then, in a kind voice, he asked her what he could do for her.

Eileen told him that she wanted to obtain an interview with Mrs. Roosevelt. The President called his wife over to him and explained the situation. Although the First Lady refused to grant Eileen a formal interview, she graciously agreed to let Eileen spend the following day with her, from morning until sunset. Once again Eileen got an interview with a First Lady that could not be called an interview. She had taken a "stroll in a garden" with Mrs. Hoover; now she was about to "spend a day" with Mrs. Roosevelt.

Eileen's historic day began early the next morning. She arrived at the hotel while Mrs. Roosevelt was still taking a before-breakfast swim in the hotel pool. After breakfast the party traveled to Balboa Park for a tour of the exposition. The members of the group, including Eileen and her new friend, a Secret Service man, rode through the park in little electric carts. Eileen proved helpful when the First Lady announced that she wanted to buy some gifts for her family. Eileen knew where the best shops were, and she thrilled several proprietors when she steered Mrs. Roosevelt into their stores.

Eileen found the First Lady to be a thoughtful, courteous person. She said that Mrs. Roosevelt thanked everyone who did anything for her during that day. Eileen decided that she was also a frugal person, for Eileen noted that someone—perhaps Mrs. Roosevelt herself?—had mended one of the stockings she was wearing.

Eileen always expressed admiration for Mrs. Roosevelt, but never wild enthusiasm. My mother reserved her highest praise for President Roosevelt—her rescuer and protector, "the man with the radiant smile."

*

Eileen's initiative enabled her to spend a day with Mrs. Roosevelt. Over the years that same enterprising spirit often helped her in her career. On one assignment, however, she was stymied. She tried and tried to obtain news from a certain person, with no success. When she finally achieved her goal, her success was not due to her own initiative, but to the help she received from an unexpected source.

When Eileen went to work at the *Union* in 1930, one of her jobs was to write about the social life of the "service set." As San Diego was a Navy town, she was supposed to contact the wives of the high-ranking naval officers in the area and give their social activities special coverage.

Eileen followed through with her usual success until Captain and Mrs. Chester Nimitz came to town, in 1931. Later, of course, during World War II, Chester Nimitz would be known as Admiral Nimitz, Commander in Chief, U.S. Pacific Fleet and Pacific Ocean Areas. In 1931 he was not yet famous. He was, however, the new commander of thirty-five deactivated destroyers at the San Diego Destroyer Base, so Eileen knew she should contact Mrs. Nimitz and start writing up her parties.

Mrs. Nimitz was uninterested. She was very nice and very polite, but she made it clear to Eileen that she wouldn't be giving any parties if she could help it. She went on to say that if she *had* to put on some kind of social event, she doubted that anyone would want to read about it.

Eileen told her editor. "Try again," he said.

Eileen called Mrs. Nimitz again, and got the same response. It became a kind of game for Eileen. Every so often during the next year she would call Mrs. Nimitz, and each time she would receive the same negative, but sweetly expressed answer. Finally Eileen gave up.

In 1933, toward the end of the school year at San Diego State, Everett told Eileen that he would like to give a little party in their home for some of his favorite students. "I would like to include that nice little Navy wife," he said, "that sailor's wife, who's been auditing my art class all year."

"What little Navy wife?" asked Eileen. "What sailor's wife?"

"Her name's Mrs. Nimitz," Everett replied. "She's a very good artist. I've enjoyed having her in my class this year."

After it was verified that Everett's "Mrs. Nimitz" was indeed the captain's wife whom Eileen had been chasing for so long, Eileen asked Everett, "Why on earth did you think her husband was a sailor?"

"Oh," he said, "when she first came to my class, I asked her what her husband did. She told me he was in the Navy, so I assumed he was a sailor."

After that, after Mrs. Nimitz discovered that Eileen was the wife of her art professor, Everett Jackson, Mrs. Nimitz' attitude changed. From then on she tried her best to provide Eileen with news. When Captain Nimitz and Everett met, they took to each other right away. They were both Texans, after all. One day my parents and I spent several pleasant hours with the Nimitz family in their living quarters. I was not quite five years old, but I vividly remember our visit. The Nimitz family, including their little toddler daughter, lived on board a ship that was moored at the Destroyer Base. I was fascinated. I had never met anyone who lived on a ship before.

On the Eve of War

On December 10, 1939, Eileen began her editorial: "As this appalling year closes ..." Her words expressed the feelings of many San Diegans. The war in Europe had begun the previous September, and Americans were edgy.

Had there been no war news to worry her, Eileen would have felt content. The final two years of the thirties decade were happy ones for her. By 1938 she and Everett had begun camping in Baja California in their spare time. Their friend Lowell Houser, of the Chapala days, had joined the art department at San Diego State and was now back in their life. They had acquired a group of close friends—creative types, for the most part—with whom they often socialized. They enjoyed the company of people like Lowell, the painters Marius and Margot Rocle, the sculptor Donal Hord, the author Max Miller and his wife, Margaret. Max, that former reporter on *The San Diego Sun*—the man who had arrived to back up young Eileen when she was interviewing the Russian ballerina Pavlova—had quit his job at the paper years before and written a best seller, *I Cover the Waterfront*. He had become famous overnight for that one charming little book, and he had then gone on to write other charming books. My father always said that Max had the soul of a poet. But when I was little, I wasn't aware of his poetic soul. To me he was a big, cranky bear. His gruff manner terrified me. It turned out Max felt nervous around children. By the time I was seventeen, we had become the best of friends.

In the summer of 1938 my parents and I camped for several days at Laguna Hanson, up in the mountains of Baja California. The lake, Laguna Hanson, was only eighty miles south of the border, but the road to it was so bad it took a full day of driving to get there. Accompanying us on that trip were two other close friends of Eileen and Everett's, John and Harriett Wimmer, and my special companion and fellow ten-year-old, Mimi Borthwick.

The Wimmers wanted to enjoy the experience. They tried not to panic when our car developed vapor lock in the middle of nowhere on the way south, and they did their best to adjust to the rigors of camp life after we reached the lake. But they never appeared really at ease until days later, when we recrossed the border back into the United States. They were city folk, not campers. Harriett, who would eventually become a renowned landscape architect, did admire the setting—the tall pine trees and great white boulders surrounding the peaceful mountain lake.

The Wimmers loved talking about the trip after they got home. They were proud to have survived a camping trip, but, as far as I know, they never camped again. They remained close friends of my parents, however, for the rest of their lives. My mother looked up to Harriett, and admired her exquisite taste. She considered Harriett to be her mentor.

Eileen had a moment of triumph, though, some weeks after the camping trip, when *she* became the mentor. One day Harriett called Eileen, nearly in tears. John, a finicky eater, had been asking for pancakes "like the ones Eileen made on the camping trip." Harriett said she had been trying every pancake recipe she owned, but nothing was satisfying John. She begged Eileen to share her "gourmet recipe."

Eileen, whose cooking skills were rudimentary at that time, had to admit that her pancakes came out of a box. The "secret ingredient," she told Harriett, was the fresh mountain air. John and Harriett remained unconvinced. They raved about Eileen's pancakes for years afterwards.

The next summer my parents and I returned to Laguna Hanson and camped for a week in that beautiful, secluded spot. Our fellow campers in 1939 were Lowell Houser, the Rocles, the author Judy Van der Veer, and her eleven-year-old niece, Mary Lou Van der Veer.

As in 1938, we saw many sheep and rattlesnakes during our

stay, and my father caught more fish than he could count. That year a Mexican cowboy was living in a little cabin across the lake. Occasionally he would visit us to chat. Otherwise we had the place to ourselves. The adults in our party must have found it difficult to think about the possibility of war when they were spending a week in paradise.

Marius Rocle painted a marvelous painting of the camp, Judy Van der Veer wrote an article about it that was printed in *The Christian Science Monitor*, and Eileen described it in a social editorial called "Last Day in Summer Camp." She wrote:

> Vacation is almost over and we have to show for it a tan which is wind burned rather than fashionably toast brown, nails and hands which are darkly eloquent of the fact that we have done our share of pot handling over the open camp fire, hair so smoke-scented that we hesitate to submit it to the shampoo operator, whose immaculate world seems as remote today as those constellations we have been sleeping under. It had taken only one al fresco week to erase our urban varnish, which, by necessity, we must apply again before we can return with any decency to a roofed world.
>
> We have re-learned a lot of things about camping, about life in the great outdoors. We have learned again how to keep butter without refrigeration; how to land, filet and fry a three-pound bass; how to sleep on the ground of unrelenting hardness; how to assume indifference when a rattlesnake is killed in camp. We know now that our dispositions are at lowest ebb before morning coffee and that they stubbornly improve with the day, allowing the community good-will to reach a height at the after-supper camp fire that invites all members to join in jolly, if off-pitched, song. We know now what supplies to take: Plenty of coffee, green tomatoes, firm avocados and melons which are allowed to ripen in camp, bread wrapped

> in three layers of waxed paper; canned goods which when used satisfy whetted appetites and lighten the home-bound load, fresh milk frozen with dry ice, nails with which to make tree shelves out of the packing boxes, a great tin lard can to ant-proof perishables, clothes pins and line for the dish towels, which are boiled only when they are as black as the pots.
>
> We are amazed to see how we can adapt our city souls to the raw outdoors, how quickly we are to achieve some sort of order even in camp housekeeping. A frying pan or a cake of soap off the chosen rock is as unforgivable in camp as their misplacement would be in the home. It's unforgivable, too, in camp to waste water, to walk carelessly around the camp stove … to leave on walks or out-of-camp excursions before the dishes are done, to complain about camp discomforts, to diet for beauty or even health's sake.
>
> Vacation is nearly over and as we pack the equipment we observe that we have let the enchanted days slip by without writing one letter on the stationery which we had packed in the suitcase with such admirable intentions a week ago, that we have not touched the mending, which we high-mindedly brought along, that we have not even read more than one book in the little library we tucked in the car corners the day we started out. Nothing accomplished. Days exquisitely wasted. Now we know that we deserve leisure since we seem to be able to spend it so effortlessly—so unintelligently.

In the first draft of her editorial Eileen did not mention a rattlesnake. Everett read her editorial and liked it, but he complained that she had made that week sound too enjoyable. Her words, he said, would surely encourage vast numbers of Americans to descend upon Laguna Hanson. It would then be ruined for civilization-hating, nature-loving campers like himself.

"Oh, I'll fix that!" Eileen promised him, and in went the sentence about the snake killed in camp. In the weeks that followed, Eileen received many compliments on her story. But after complimenting her, she reported, those people invariably added, "I'm sure it's a beautiful place, but I certainly wouldn't want to go there, with all those rattlesnakes around!"

*

During the last two years of the 1930s Eileen continued to produce an upbeat society page. On December 11, 1938, she added a column, "Tips for Teens," to the women's section. The "Tips for Teens" clippings that have turned up among her papers do not reveal whether the "mature" Eileen ever advised any of her teenage readers to kiss their dates.

As the situation in Europe grew more tense in 1939, and then exploded into war, Eileen kept on turning out cheerful columns and editorials. Optimism came naturally to her, and her own life was going smoothly. It was hard for her to think about the situation in Europe, and about the effect that situation might have someday on the people she knew.

She devoted one editorial that spring to finger bowls, another to after-dinner entertainment at private parties. In July she advised her readers to "skip the surprises," because most people don't like surprise parties, or any kind of surprise, for that matter. She quoted Emerson as saying that life is a series of surprises, but "somehow we never get used to them." In September she discussed scrapbooks, in November telephones. She wrote all those lighthearted editorials, and then came that phrase in December: "As this appalling year closes …"

Throughout 1940 Eileen's columns and editorials varied in tone. In March of 1940 she wrote an amusing editorial on a subject that had personal meaning to her. In "Did You Ever Survive Moving Day?" she described her family's recent move to a new house, a house that would shelter and enchant her for the next fifty-six years. In her editorial she said:

> We got all the moving advice we could from our

> transient friends ... They recommended first a reliable moving van ...
>
> Things might not have been so bad if we had taken the first recommendation of hiring a reliable van with professional movers, but we were only moving down the hill from our former abode and we fancied we could go ... with our household gear ... on our backs. For us, as for the old timers who didn't know what it was to have a great modern van, moving day was a day of confession, of betrayal. Our tendency to save too much, our eccentricities as revealed by such things as lampshades, our decoration failures were piteously revealed to those who cared to watch our forlorn parade.

The new home was unique. It was not just a house; it was a romantic Spanish palace. It was also a challenge. The house was hard to get to and hard to live in. It was the kind of place that would daunt most people, but to Eileen and Everett it was the house of their dreams.

Another artist, Leslie Lee, had designed and built it in the twenties. He and his wife, an authority on Native American lore and a writer of children's books, had entertained my parents in that house in 1928. Ten years later, during the Depression, the Lees had found themselves unable to keep up their mortgage payments, and they had lost the house. It sat empty for two years, overgrown with vines, abandoned, unloved.

Mr. Lee's architectural masterpiece clung to a hillside high above San Diego's Mission Valley, a valley that was silent and undeveloped back in 1940. A person had to walk down thirty-six tile steps to get to the front door. There were two floors below that level, and one above. The house had a wilderness of trees and plants surrounding it. It also had five balconies and an artist's studio forty feet long, thirty feet wide and eighteen feet high, with a huge north window. Probably the most unusual feature of the house was the massive wooden door at the western end of the studio. It led outside but opened onto nothing. If a person were to walk through it, he or she would plunge to the ground a full floor below. One of Eileen and Everett's first acts upon moving into their new home was to lock that door!

Eileen and Everett's previous home was a comfortable, two-story house up the street from the Lees' house. My parents' first San Diego house had enough bedrooms and baths to satisfy them, but it lacked a studio for Everett, where he could paint. For years he had used a corner of the master bedroom as his studio. He and Eileen had bought the house from her parents in the early thirties, and by 1940 they had paid off the mortgage. When they found out that the house down the street was available, they had an unmortgaged, comfortable house to offer the Homeowner Loan Corporation in exchange for that rambling, four-story, difficult-to-live-in palace.

Eileen and Everett did some research before trading their conventional house for the unconventional one. They sought the advice of their artistic friends and of some of their practical relatives. To their surprise, several of the "imaginative" people they queried said things like, "Oh, I don't know. It's pretty big, and it will be hard to furnish and to keep up. And all those steps! Are you sure you want to do this?"

Eileen's builder father, however, assured them that the house was structurally sound (he had known the contractor who built it), and he advised them to go ahead with the exchange. Eileen's practical, businessman brother advised the same thing. He said he would never live in a house like that himself, but he thought it would be perfect for Eileen and Everett.

The decision made, we left our old house, sad to leave behind Everett's two murals, one in the downstairs bathroom, one in the breakfast room. But the closet door in my bedroom was too important to me to leave behind. My father had painted a scene on it that depicted all the characters in the stories he had told me over the years. Eileen discovered a door in the new house that looked as though it might fit the closet in my old bedroom. Everett measured it. It did fit, and a door exchange took place. To me that exchange was just as important as the one involving the houses. My painted door, like so many other items, was carried down by hand to the new house, but no one would ever have called it a "decoration failure."

*

After Eileen and Everett had moved into their palace, and had begun building new rock walls and expanding old terraces, they received a letter from the former owner, Mrs. Lee. In it she said:

> We passed the house on the Mission Valley ride one night, and it was lighted from tip to toe and looked so gay. I am sure you will give this old house a better time than we, as you will make it more colorful and joyous. I think it was lonely much of the time when we were there.

In August of 1940, Eileen wrote an editorial that charmed her readers. In her August 18 editorial, "It's Hard to Forget the Old House," she said:

> The house we used to live in is only a few doors from where we live today and we wish it weren't. Making a move from a house you've built from the ground up, paid for in agonizingly slow installments, loved but outgrown, is wrench enough, but to have it near enough to look you reproachfully in the face every day is more than some members of our family can stand. It was endurable when it stood empty because somehow it still seemed to belong to us, but now that the deserted child has been adopted by new owners who are willing to shower on it as much affection as we used to give it, the nostalgia seems unbearable. We personally could have shut our eyes on it and lost ourselves in plans for the new house. We could have resisted the appeal of the old walls in adapting familiar furnishings to the new setting. To discourage insistent memories of pleasant personal

features of the abandoned habitat—the little breakfast room mural, for instance—we would have schooled ourselves to think of the possibilities of the new house. But it takes more Spartan "on with the new" courage than we can muster to ignore the sentiment of the younger members of our family who insist on pointing out the charm of and the change in the old house. When we come home night after night from the office to find the dejected dog sitting lonesomely on the terrace of the old house and when we are greeted daily by the 12-year-old with fresh accounts of what has gone on at the old address, we find it impossible to pass it up like any other house on the street.

"The new people have got a lamp and table where we used to have the old love seat," gossiped Miss Pigtails, who seemed to have done some, what we hope was imperceptible, snooping in our absence. To our surprise and annoyance, we found we were interested. We even, incredible though it seems, heard ourselves asking what else the new owners had installed before we admonished her not to be peeping in the neighbor's windows.

Two days later the report concerned the garden. The weeding out, though in the interest of a new and neater yard, offended the young reporter. She regretted the passing of some ivy on the chimney, particularly when she remembered that the leaves would turn color soon.

The last straw was when the curtains went up. Curtains are so personal, so intimate, such shutters-out.

"They've got curtains up now," announced the little lady, resignedly. Now that they, crisp and fresh, were up she could no longer claim the old house. They were the finishing touch, the final gesture which locked her out. A nice little girl might take a peek in a big open window without pricking her conscience but to peer beyond curtains was unthinkable.

We like the neighbors who live in our old house and with no idea of snooping we are going to make an old fashioned neighborly call one of these days. When we mentioned that prospect in the family circle, the youngest member said she didn't believe she'd go. She might be shown her old room which was her nursery 10 years ago and she just couldn't stand that.

Considering our sentimental family, we've decided that if ever we move again—and heaven forbid—we'll move to the other part of town.

Eileen and Everett never did move again. As Mrs. Lee had predicted, they made their new house a joyous place. They filled it with beautiful objects, and Everett painted four murals on its interior walls. He also painted the face and figure of a woman on one of the bedroom doors. As usual the woman in his painting looked like Eileen.

My parents negotiated those stairs to the end of their lives. At ninety, Everett was still bounding up and down them. At ninety-four, he moved slowly, but still could make it to the street unaided. During the last years of her life Eileen had more trouble, although as she often pointed out, it was her good leg that pained her when she climbed the stairs, not the "miracle leg."

During World War II, and for some time afterwards, Eileen and Everett rented the lower two floors of the house. They were able to turn that area into a rental unit because the house had two kitchens.

Over the years five weddings took place in the studio. The first was in 1940, when Eileen's cousin was the groom. The last was in 1979. Then, in 1990, the garden served as the setting for a ceremony. Eileen and Everett's great-granddaughter was christened in front of the fountain that friends had presented to them in recognition of their fiftieth wedding anniversary.

The minute Eileen moved into her new house, she wanted to

give it a name. At first, for obvious reasons, she thought she and Everett should name it Vertical Acres. Then she considered Holly Hill, because of the wild California holly that bloomed on the hillside each December. Neither name really took. Finally, in 1949, the Texas author and educator J. Frank Dobie named the house, and his name is the one it still goes by today.

When he visited my parents on a summer afternoon in 1949, they told him that at night they often heard coyotes howl down in the valley below. (Now, of course, one hears only the roar of traffic.) J. Frank Dobie was famous for his legends of the Southwest. He liked coyotes, and he was tickled to think that in an essentially urban setting one could still hear a coyote's howl.

"Why then," Mr. Dobie said, "you should call this place the House of the Coyote's Song."

And the House of the Coyote's Song is what the family has called it ever since.

*

After writing that March 1940 editorial on "Moving Day," Eileen grew more serious. On May 26, 1940, she produced a somber editorial. Apparently for one week in May, as Hitler's troops charged across France, San Diegans faltered. They lost their social nerve. Eileen's editorial was headed "They Don't Feel Like Partying Now." In it she said:

> Last week there was a social slack, a decided dearth of amusing affairs, of jolly party plotting, and the reason society gave for the recess did not suggest a desire to relax but a mood at once desperate and dejected. Society, frankly, was headline jittery ... We've had serious days before—deep business depressions and natural disasters, but nothing in our more than a decade of social scribbling has ever so effectively dampened society's spirits as the news that was made a continent and an ocean away.

However, Eileen couldn't help adding:

> But … the social lull among the horrified spectators will pass … There will be parties on the social page again even when the front page is dedicated to disheartening headlines … our spirits will bounce back enough to allow us to find pleasure again in harmless little social "doings."

In her June 16 editorial her tone again was somber. She commented on the number of Navy weddings currently taking place in San Diego, weddings that suggested a "war-time rush," even though America was not at war. She wrote, "We are forced to conclude that these dreadful and cheerless days … far from dissuading those who are altar-bound, actually rush them into matrimony."

*

During the months that led up to America's entrance into World War II, Eileen continued to lead a productive, satisfying life. She was growing closer to her readers; she was starting to think of them as "family." She was having fun with her house. Every now and then someone came to town for her to interview. On July 25, 1941, the *Union* published a long article she wrote after talking with Lady Halifax, the wife of Britain's ambassador to the United States.

Eileen's interview with Lady Halifax is interesting, but of interest, too, is the short news article on the back of the clipping about Lady Halifax. It is an AP article out of San Francisco, dated July 24, 1941, that said:

> Taking a tip from the British evacuation at Dunkerque, the U.S. navy is organizing small-boat operators at a dozen California coastal towns to patrol Pacific waters in wartime.
>
> The navy will depend on these boats to locate enemy periscopes, small craft attempted landings,

> enemy aircraft bound inland … in fact to be on the lookout for any trouble that might develop …
>
> Small-craft operators and their crews are being inducted into the naval reserve on a voluntary basis, the 12th naval district announced tonight.

Apparently, some people were thinking ahead. The people at the twelfth naval district who organized those patrols must not have been too surprised on December 7 of that year.

The War Years

On December 7, 1941, America found itself at war. San Diegans were stunned. They shouldn't have been. For over two years their city had been preparing for war. Since 1939 aircraft workers had been pouring into San Diego, along with military personnel.

After America entered the war, more and more defense workers appeared in San Diego, and more and more members of the military. The population of San Diego had already jumped from around two hundred thousand in 1940 to three hundred thousand in mid-1941. Two years later it was approaching half a million. When one ventured downtown during the war, one saw hundreds of white caps. Sailors were everywhere. There were so many sailors on the streets of San Diego a person might wonder who was manning the ships at sea.

As the months passed in 1942, Eileen's life began to change. The first change probably sounds unimportant compared to what was happening around the country and around the world. Nevertheless, it seemed important to Eileen: she lost her household help. That meant she had to learn to cook. All her married life she had had someone to cook for her—in Mexico, in Texas, and in San Diego, when first her mother and then a series of housekeepers had done the cooking.

Of course Eileen could cook a little. She wasn't completely helpless in the kitchen, and in recent years she had proved she could prepare food on a camping trip. She could fry fish, for example, and she could make pancakes. However, in early 1942 the day-in, day-out kind of cooking at which most wives excelled was a mystery to her. She had assumed that she would always have help in her home as long as she kept working, but suddenly there was no help to be had. In 1942 the maids in town disappeared like magic into the factory Consolidated Aircraft.

Eileen, as usual, faced her new challenge with a positive spirit. She refused to produce boring meals. If she was going to have to cook, she told her family, she would do it right. Out came the cookbooks, and the wine and herbs—a lot of wine and herbs. Soon my father and I acknowledged that, in spite of her previous inexperience, and in spite of wartime rationing and shortages, she had become a gourmet cook.

Her next problem involved the house: it was too big. It had seemed the right size when a housekeeper was in residence, but now it overwhelmed Eileen.

Each weekday morning she would travel by streetcar to her office downtown. Then, at five, she would ride home on the streetcar. It was so crowded at that hour she often had to stand. To make matters worse, many people pushed and shoved in order to get seats. Eileen, at least, could vent her irritation in print. In her September 27, 1942, editorial, "Courtesy in Wartime," she said:

> There seems to be a marked degeneration lately in street car and waiting line courtesy. We do not mean that tempers are short, for everyone seems resigned to the wartime inconveniences ... It is not conscious, malicious discourtesy, just lack of courtesy. Blame it on to the war crowds, the war rush and the weariness of the war workers.

When she reached the streetcar stop nearest to her home, she would get off, buy groceries at the corner grocery store, and return home to cook and clean. By evening she was exhausted. My father and I did what we could to help around the house (our chores were to wash and dry the dinner dishes and occasionally to vacuum), but Eileen was the one who worked the hardest.

In an editorial called "Leading Double Lives," Eileen addressed the problems faced by women like herself—women in wartime who were trying to care for a home while holding down a job outside the home. She wrote:

> An eight-hour day for women at the factory or office meeting people, doing things, keeping alert, getting paid for your time is, to many temperaments, stimulating, and even fun. And most of us who have done it through the years have defended our "careers" to the housewives by emphatically insisting: "we wouldn't trade our jobs, with all their problems, for your dishes three times a day, bed making and dusting." That was in the old days when there were two roles from which women could choose. Today the confirmed householder, she who prefers her four-walled kingdom has through economic or patriotic impulse entered our world, and we through necessity, having lost our full or part-time help, have been forced to invade her domestic domain.
>
> ... If we two-job women can't work out an efficiency program, a technique of shortcuts which will allow us to serve our employer competently without losing order and beauty in our lives at home, we will have failed on the home front, that second line of defense.
>
> From personal experience and from the experiences of friends who have reared families while holding down jobs away from home, we have gathered some ideas which might be worth passing on to those who are about to lead double lives for the first time.
>
> Most of the experienced combination careerist-homemakers agree that the first fundamental rule is "don't bring your work home with you." Concentrate on the job, give it everything you've got, forget about the supper menu or the unwashed breakfast dishes at home until quitting time. Then turn your back with that same deliberate indifference on the office or factory job and face the

home front.

Eileen went on to offer advice on how to strip one's "home and life down to wartime essentials," how to shop and plan ahead, and, perhaps as a little nudge to my father and me, how to press the family into service. She continued her editorial, saying:

> The housewife who works … particularly in war times or times of stress, should not be the only one held responsible for the smooth running of the household. Other members of the family should share the responsibility.

Eileen must not have followed her own good advice, for all of a sudden the pressure of her new life got to her. One day she woke up and discovered that the fingers on both her hands were painful and swollen. She panicked; she was afraid she would never be able to type again.

Her doctor, an old friend who had once worked with her as a reporter on *The San Diego Sun*, told her, "You're under too much stress. Take a drink at night. You need to relax. Your kind of arthritis will get well if you take a little drink."

When Eileen protested that she only drank at parties, and then not very much, her friend exclaimed, "You're a reporter, for God's sake! All reporters drink! But it doesn't have to be hard liquor. Take a little sherry while you're cooking dinner. It'll help; you'll see."

Eileen's doctor was a graduate of Stanford Medical School. Whether his professors at Stanford had taught him to prescribe sherry for arthritic fingers, Eileen never knew, but the prescription worked. She began sipping sherry at night as she cooked, and the arthritis disappeared.

The house, however, was still too big. By that time Eileen and Everett had begun hearing from their friends about the house. Their friends told them it was unpatriotic for three people to live in a place that big when families were coming to town needing housing. "Your house has two kitchens," one friend reminded them. "You should rent the lower half."

Eileen and Everett agreed that their friends had a point. New people were arriving in San Diego every day, and the city was about to run out of places to house them. Many San Diegans were renting rooms to defense workers and their families, and to the families of servicemen.

Eileen had even written an editorial on the subject. It was entitled "Hospitality Honor Roll," and it began:

> Giving up the guest room has become a patriotic duty in cities such as San Diego, where defense industries attracting large increases in population have made the housing situation acute.
>
> San Diego, which has the tradition of the "it is yours" generosity of the Spanish dons, is opening its homes to the … newcomers.
>
> We can name many to the honor roll …

Eileen then proceeded to list some of the generous San Diegans who were responding to the housing crisis by opening "their hearts and their doors."

After writing an editorial like that, and after listening to her friends, Eileen decided she and Everett should act. After all, they had two whole floors to offer. It would be most unpatriotic of them to go on rattling around in that big house when worthy strangers needed homes. Also, if they rented those lower two floors, they would have two less floors to clean.

Early in 1943 Eileen and Everett began renting the lower apartment. Over a period of eleven years a succession of renters occupied the apartment. My parents kept on renting it long after the housing crisis had ended. They did that, they explained, because they had grown used to the setup, and because their tenants were such interesting people.

*

In some notes Eileen wrote about the war years, she described the Christmas season of 1942. Because of gas rationing, she said, people were unable to travel very far to parties. As a result, many traditional events were canceled. Eileen wrote that the Christmas parties of 1942 were "regional, not county wide," that there were "no lighted outdoor Christmas trees," and that "social life, such as it was, took place behind dark shades."

During the last months of 1942, San Diegans still feared a Japanese attack. Air-raid wardens, which included Everett, patrolled their neighborhoods each evening to make sure that everyone's shades were drawn.

In a November 1942 editorial, Eileen wrote about the San Diego women volunteers whose job it was to look skyward, for four hours at a stretch, and "record the flight of every plane, army, navy, commercial and student trainer in the air lest an enemy plane slip through unobserved."

Eileen's mother was one of those ground observers. She had been a member of the aircraft warning service since Pearl Harbor. My grandmother was an active volunteer worker and club woman during the war. In 1941-43 she served as president of the San Diego County Federation of Women's Clubs. Later she worked with the USO as chairman of its advisory committee. Women like her kept the USO constantly in the news. It was a busy, humming place throughout the war.

*

During the war years, Eileen tried to put out a cheerful women's section. She succeeded. She filled her "Tete-a-Tete" columns with news about births, engagements, the arrival of house guests, and the parties given for the house guests. She wrote about christening parties and about freshmen (all of them, female) going off to college. In 1942 she began inviting local women to contribute articles to the women's page. She called her new series "Guest Artists on Assignments for Fun."

Mostly, however, Eileen and her staff wrote up weddings. They had many to write up. They tried to make the weddings sound as normal as the ones they had covered before the war. This often took ingenuity, for as Eileen commented in her notes, "Sometimes brides from out of town would arrive with elaborate wedding dresses but no wedding guests to watch them go down the aisles of local chapels."

Perhaps Eileen succeeded too well in producing a cheerful women's section. Perhaps someone complained that her words didn't reflect the grim reality of war. She may have been responding to such a complaint when she wrote one of her wartime editorials, in which she begged her readers to "read between the lines." She said that if the social columns sounded too frivolous, it was because the reporter was "deliberately [using] restraint in telling the story." She went on to say:

> Take those paragraphs concerning orders and new commissions which fill our pages … Do the new posts, the farewell parties sound exciting to you in print? That's because you don't know, or forget, the high courage … the long, long days of waiting, the painful new adjustments involved in every single notice.
>
> … Our columns were never so filled with romance, with engagements, [and] impressive church ceremonies … Those stories, too, are deceiving … Often before the story is printed the bridegroom has gone and the bride, home with her parents, has to send their most precious "press clippings" to his faraway post.
>
> Don't mistake it—these are war weddings. Happy and enduring, we hope, but for the most part, hasty. They make the columns June-like the year round, but it's only "youth's primeval dauntlessness" which keeps the march to the altar endless.
>
> … We have no trouble getting news these days and we make a conscious effort to keep it from appearing depressing, but it's not really so merry as it sounds. We invite you to read between the lines.

*

The war began to affect Eileen and Everett's group of friends. Lowell Houser, who was a bachelor and several years younger than Everett, was drafted. The Army released him when he suffered a mild heart attack during basic training. Max Miller, a Navy veteran from World War I, was commissioned in the Navy in the spring of 1942, and served for three years. As a naval officer on active duty, he wrote three books about the war.

The war went on, and Eileen and Everett, like so many Americans, began to lose relatives. Eileen lost a favorite first cousin, a flyer in the Pacific. Everett lost a nephew on a tanker that was sunk in the North Atlantic. On June 8, 1944, in Normandy, another of Everett's nephews was killed. Two months later the husband of one of Everett's nieces died fighting in a different part of France. Eileen said that she and Everett dreaded phone calls from Texas, for the news was always so sad.

But finally, in August of 1945, the war did end. On Sunday, December 16, 1945, Eileen wrote in her "Yuletide Cheerio" column:

> Merry Christmas—without apologies this year. For the first Christmas since 1940 … the world can celebrate festively, can light up the Christmas trees indoors and out … can raise the cup of cheer in jolly toasts and the voice in lighthearted song without rationalizing as it did from 1941 through 1944 that such abandon was to lift morale …

To Eileen "the world" obviously meant Americans, but everyone understood what she was saying. The war was over. People could make happy plans for the future, and Eileen could write cheerful columns again, "without apologies."

Some Tricks of the Trade and a Surprising Move

Back in the thirties, Eileen had begun collecting information about the people whose names appeared in her column. It was not incriminating information, just their current address and phone number, the names of their children, their children's birthdays, and so on. Eileen had a separate file card for each family, and she kept the cards, in alphabetical order, in a large metal box. She was uncharacteristically neat where those cards were concerned. She knew she had to be, for they were cards she used every day in her work. She had to know where to find a name when she needed it.

Each morning she would call a number of people in the file to get news. In those days the "lady of the house" was usually home in the morning, eager to chat. In a period of weeks Eileen would have called everyone in the file, from *A* to *Z*. Then she would start over.

Of course she called other people, too, people who were not in her file, when she was after a story. Also, she checked in with some women every few days, if they were good sources of news and/or her close friends. Many times she called her file people out of order. For instance, a *W* file person who was planning a wedding might receive a call from Eileen on the day when Eileen was officially calling the *B*s.

As the years passed, the file grew larger and larger, for Eileen's column was always an inclusive one. If newcomers arrived in town who seemed both well bred and sincerely interested in their new community, Eileen would add their names to her column and to her file.

On one occasion her system of calling San Diegans enabled

her to save a life. When she telephoned a certain woman, the woman answered the phone and gasped, "I think I'm dying, Eileen! I've just managed to crawl to the phone. Please help!"

Eileen told her friend to hang up immediately. Eileen said that she would call that woman's daughter—or, if she couldn't reach her, someone else—and get help. Eileen reached the daughter, the daughter got medical help, and the woman's life was saved. She had been severely dehydrated and very close to death. She had felt too weak to make a phone call, to pick up the phone and dial, but when it rang somehow she had roused herself enough to answer it.

She was a matter-of-fact person, known for her sharp, amusing comments. She knew about the card file, and after her recovery she said to Eileen, "Thank God you were calling the *G*s that morning! I wouldn't be alive today if you'd been on any other letter!"

*

Eileen was personally acquainted with most of the people in her file. Many were from old San Diego families. She knew that one man's mother was a Jessop; that another man's wife was a Fletcher; that Mrs. Henry B. Clark was Lena Sefton Wakefield when she founded the Charity Ball. Eileen also knew which San Diegans were descended from President Ulysses S. Grant. She kept all this information in her head, but she did need the file cards in order to keep track of the children in a family.

Eileen was famous for not taking notes at a party. People were always amazed at her memory. She must have astounded some of the women she called, those who were unaware of her card system.

"Good morning!" she might say to a woman in the file. "This is Eileen. Do you have any family news to report? How are Johnny, Joan, and Harry? Isn't Harry about to have a birthday?"

It was true that my mother never took notes, or later talked into a tape recorder, at a party. She could remember what the women were wearing at most of the parties she attended. She did, however, write up some of the larger parties and all of the balls ahead of time. She would call the women who were planning to attend a certain large party or ball and get their dress descriptions beforehand. Then she would write the story up and hand it in. After that she would go to the event, to direct her photographer in his photo-taking, and to make sure that the women had worn what they'd said they would. Sometimes the women wore something else, and that would cause Eileen to dash to a phone, to get the paper to change her story.

One day an elderly lady, a sweet, amiable person, promised Eileen that that night she would be wearing a long blue-satin dress at her wedding-anniversary party. The lady was dear, and she had the best of intentions, but she had grown a little vague. Eileen turned in her copy and appeared at the party, relaxed and ready to enjoy a pleasant evening. The honored guests, a couple prominent in the community, were standing in the receiving line, and the wife was wearing a long red-velvet dress.

"But Mrs.—," Eileen exclaimed, as she reached her friend, "I thought you'd be wearing blue tonight!"

"Oh," said the sweet little woman, looking down in surprise at her bright-red dress, "aren't I?"

*

Eileen was usually able to phone in last-minute changes to her stories, but back in the thirties it was impossible to make a major change on a Saturday night. She knew that at a certain point on Saturday any copy she handed in for the Sunday edition was going to be printed, no matter what.

In those days Eileen and her staff often wrote up weddings ahead of time, especially big elaborate ones. They would describe the bride's gown and bridal bouquet, the bridesmaids' dresses, and the flowers in the church. They would also describe what happened at the wedding, or what they assumed would happen, since most weddings were pretty much alike. Then they would turn their copy in.

On one memorable occasion Eileen wrote up a large Saturday-evening wedding ahead of time. Her story was to come out in the paper the next morning. In later years Eileen remembered that her description of the bride and the bride's flowers went somewhat like this: "The blush of her cheek matched the blush of the roses in her bouquet, as she walked down the aisle on her father's arm."

"Ah," said Eileen years later, "we really wrote 'em up in those days!"

Eileen turned her copy in for the Sunday edition and went to the wedding, pleased to have written such a splendid account. The bride made it to the church that night, but the groom never showed. The bridal party and the wedding guests waited and waited. When it finally became evident that the groom was not going to appear, the bride's frantic father called the *Union*, shouting, "Stop the presses! Stop the presses!"

At that hour the presses could not be stopped, or they could have been, but for a price that did not bear mentioning. Even the bride's well-to-do father could not go that high. The *Union*'s solution was to print a little boxed message on the front page of the Sunday edition that said something to the effect of: "Please ignore the lead story in Eileen Jackson's column today."

Inside the paper, in the women's section, was the column that naturally everyone turned to first of all that morning, the column in which Eileen had said, "The blush of her cheek matched the blush of the roses …"

It turned out the groom had gone to visit his old girlfriend the afternoon of the wedding, to say good-bye. She, vengeful creature that she was, had slipped a "Mickey" into his drink. He had lost consciousness, and had remained unconscious until the following morning.

But the story had a happy ending. A year or so later the young woman who had been left at the altar and her no-show bridegroom appeared in Eileen's office. They told her they had just gotten married. They had "worked things out," they said, and they wanted her to know.

I don't know if the couple asked her to write up their real wedding, which they described as a "simple little ceremony." If

Eileen did write it up, at least she knew she was describing an event that had actually taken place.

*

When the war was over, Eileen's social page returned to normal. People were ready to have fun again. Social activity picked up in all parts of the county. Eileen and her staff were kept busy recording one party after another.

For some years Eileen had had several women working with her to put out the society section—a club editor, a woman who wrote about the service set, and others. The society writers on the *Union* got along well together. Eileen's favorite members of the group were two gentle sisters with southern names, Alice Sue Hardin and Etta Mae Wallace. She considered them her friends as well as her colleagues.

Since 1939, when the Copley Press purchased *The San Diego Sun*, the *Union* writers' main competition had come from writers on *The San Diego Tribune-Sun*. (In 1950 that paper reverted to its pre-1939 name, *The Evening Tribune*.) Although Colonel Copley owned both the *Union* and the *Tribune*, the competition between the two dailies was fierce. As a child, I didn't understand that that competition was really only a game that newspaper people played in order to get their adrenaline up. Whenever I saw a certain society reporter from the *Tribune*, I grew somewhat stiff, and I greeted her with reserve. I had gathered, from hearing my mother talk, that she was "the enemy." Of course she was not the enemy at all. She was a thoughtful, kind person, and later I found that out. We became very fond of each other. In truth she and my mother were fond of each other, too; they knew they were only playing a game.

*

After the war ended, Eileen and Everett began camping again. As in the past, they headed for Baja California, carrying their food and gear in their car. At that point they had not yet considered buying a camper, for in the mid-1940s campers did not exist.

Most of Eileen's social friends in San Diego had a hard time visualizing her on a camping trip. They couldn't believe that a woman who dressed so well in the city, and who looked so happy at parties, would care to rough it in the wilds. Since they knew from her editorials that she did indeed camp, they assumed that her husband forced her to go along and that she secretly hated the experience.

In the 1940s only her family and a few close friends knew about the "gypsy Eileen," the Eileen who adored camping, who felt at home stirring a stew pot set on a grill between two rocks, the Eileen who wore strange, voluminous outfits and a kerchief on her hair. The gypsy Eileen definitely existed, however, and some of her social friends began to know her as the postwar years went by.

Eileen's life and work should have satisfied her. She was running a busy office, she was expanding her file to include many of the new people who had come to live in San Diego after the war, and she was going on camping trips again. But apparently in 1948 she grew restless. Perhaps, as in her childhood, she wanted to climb the "far-off mountain" and see what lay on the other side. If so, the *Union* should have put her in that harness her mother had fashioned. Whatever the reason, Eileen suddenly made a career change that surprised all of her friends.

Ever since *The San Diego Sun* ceased publication, in 1939, the Copley Press had dominated the San Diego newspaper scene. Other papers did exist in the area, but since they were small they offered little competition to either the *Union* or the *Tribune*. Some people complained about the fact that one man owned both of the major papers in San Diego, but most San Diegans were satisfied with the one-owner, two-paper setup.

Then John Kennedy arrived in town—Mr. John A. Kennedy, not to be confused with J.F.K. His home was in West Virginia, where he owned a chain of radio stations. But now he was branching out. In October of 1947 he bought the most successful of San Diego's smaller papers, the *San Diego Daily Journal*. He announced that he was going to turn it into a major newspaper, one that would compete with both the *Union* and the *Tribune*. The *Journal* was already a liberal paper, and it would remain so, John Kennedy said. But it would become a *great* liberal paper.

Mr. Kennedy moved his family to San Diego and bought a beautiful home for them in the city. The Kennedys were impressive. Mrs. Kennedy was a grand lady from an old West Virginia family, a stately woman, poised and gracious. The Kennedys' two older children were attending college on the East Coast when the family moved to California; the younger two lived at home with their parents. All four quickly made friends in San Diego.

John Kennedy swept into town, along with the *Journal*'s new general manager, a man named Howard Chernoff. Together they started looking for some new reporters to add to those who were already working on the *Journal*. Before long they had staffed their newspaper. Among the "new" reporters they had found were two they had snared in a raid on the *Union*: Ken Bojens, a fine sportswriter, and their prize female acquisition, Eileen.

In February of 1948 Eileen left the *Union*, after eighteen years, and accepted a job as society editor and feature writer on the *San Diego Daily Journal*.

The *Journal* Years

Many years after Eileen's move to the *Journal*, she offered an explanation for her action. She reminded one of her friends that Colonel Copley had died in 1947, and that in 1948 his son James Copley had not yet taken over the management of the Copley Press. (He would become publisher of the *Union* and the *Tribune*, and also president of the Union-Tribune Publishing Co., in 1950.) Eileen explained that she left the *Union* because she didn't want to work for the Copley Press when a Copley was not heading it. But at the time of her move, she told friends that she would make more money working for the *Journal*, and would be given "a freer hand."

When Eileen's readers learned in January of her upcoming job change, they reacted with shock. Then they began to send her letters. Some of her fans promised to switch to the *Journal*. One of those persons, her friend Lydia Grandier, wrote:

> Dear Eileen:
>
> It has been fun to see you moving about on the chess-board, as it were!
>
> ... you seem to me to be one of those gifted people who need scope and the stimulation of new atmospheres to work in ... you take your "public" with you ...

Other readers expressed a different viewpoint. One woman said:

> Dear Eileen,
>
> It does not seem right, it just will not be right for you to no longer run your page in the Union … You personally know everybody, write interestingly, and get all the news—also we like you as a person … I've taken the Union for 30 years, so could not change. It is as if you let us all down …

A number of people gave no indication what they would do—whether they would change papers or remain faithful to the *Union*—but they wished Eileen success in her new career.

She wasn't sure she had done the right thing. It was a difficult time for her. Her readers tended to be conservative. She wondered if many of them would follow her to the liberal *Journal*. She also wondered if those liberals who were already taking the *Journal* would care about social news.

Politics never interested Eileen very much. Her instincts were conservative, but she always regarded people as people; she didn't care about their political affiliations. This ability of hers to ignore politics in her dealings with people helped her as a newspaperwoman. It also enabled her to say, in a 1988 interview in San Diego's weekly paper the *Reader*, that the male political figure who had impressed her the most was Franklin Roosevelt, and that her favorite First Lady was unquestionably Pat Nixon.

"Well, I guess that will confuse everybody!" Eileen said at the time of that interview.

*

In January of 1948 Eileen may have had misgivings about her impending move to the *Journal*, but Mr. Kennedy did not. He had already begun his publicity campaign. He arranged for Eileen to pose for a photograph, and in February he had that picture of her (one of the most beautiful of her ever taken) displayed on streetcars and buses all over town. Along with the photo was the message: "Read Eileen Jackson Daily in the San Diego Journal."

He also printed the following announcement in his paper:

> The famous, the incomparable Eileen Jackson joins the Journal! San Diego has enjoyed her social pages and Tete-a-Tete Column for 18 years. Now Eileen joins the Journal to give you the finest, most sparkling Women's and Society Pages you've ever read.

On February 9 Eileen's column began running in the *Journal*. She introduced her first column, saying:

> Making a change, even one as seemingly insignificant as varying our hair-do, selling the old homestead or changing pictures over the mantel, is an emotional experience which requires some courage and imagination. Changing jobs takes its toll on the old nervous system, too …

She added, "The move has been easier because of the kindness of those of you who have wanted to follow our columns."

A great number of Eileen's readers did drop the *Union* and begin subscribing to the *Journal* because of her. She was surprised at how many made the switch. Some people even told her that they were subscribing to the *Union* and the *Journal*. They still wanted to take the *Union*, but they also wanted to read her column every day. Eileen was the successful lure that Mr. Kennedy had hoped she would be.

The *Journal* staff was young and full of enthusiasm. Eileen was one of the older members of the group, and in February of 1948 she was only forty-one. Years later she wrote in her notes:

> It was like being on a paper made up of cub reporters—not in the sense that they were inexperienced or naive, but because they were so eager and energetic. Nobody was blasé; everyone was determined to make the Journal the best paper in the city.

Eileen enjoyed working on the *Journal*. While there, she met a young reporter from North Carolina named Neil Morgan, who would eventually become her editor. She mothered her staff of brilliant youngsters, and she listened to them and counseled them as they told her about their love lives. Eileen found her new environment stimulating.

She continued to produce a snappy column, and after a while, in order to pep up her page even more, she began writing an editorial a day. Most of the editorials were short little pieces, but several were as long as the ones she had written once a week.

Reading those editorials today, one finds that while some of them offer dated advice, many of them could easily appear in a current publication. Her editorial "Fun For The Fifth Wheel" seems especially up-to-date. She wrote:

> Finding extra men to balance the dinner table seating when there are widowed or single women in the party is one of the hostess' most persistent problems.
>
> We admit that finding attractive bachelors, who are at a premium here, is a problem but why should the hostess try? What is wrong with a so-called unbalanced table? Why should unescorted women be relegated to luncheon parties and forgotten for the evening entertainment because there are not enough men to go around?

Another editorial, on the subject of weddings, seems a little dated now, but the philosophy expressed in it is ageless. Any contemporary bride could profit from reading it. It was entitled "Needed—More Common Sense" and in it Eileen said:

> Anyone who has staged a large wedding … will tell you that faithful attention to detail assures a smooth ceremony. Although we are perfectly aware of this … we still think—judging from the countless small questions which come to our desk regarding wedding etiquette—there is too much emphasis on the little things and not enough on

> fundamentals.
>
> What does it matter if the ushers wear dinner jackets before dark (considered socially incorrect) if they all happen to have them and do not own approved dark double breasted suits or cutaways and do not want to buy them for the occasion. The fundamental to consider here is "unity" so the groomsmen won't look like a company of ill-fitted recruits.
>
> What does it matter whether the guests greet the bride or the bridegroom first at the reception, whether the bride has an engagement ring or not, whether tissue paper is left in the engraved wedding announcement or removed …
>
> Those are the "little things," and oddly enough they are the ones which are worried about.
>
> We think the principals should stop being concerned about insignificant details and let common sense, reasonable economy and thoughtfulness dictate. It is "fundamental," for instance, that in making up wedding lists old friends should not be left out to make room for new ones who seem of greater social importance. It is important that the bride, although she has the say-so in wedding procedure, be thoughtful in regard to the wishes of the bridegroom and his family.
>
> What is "proper" usually is what is sensible and kind.

*

In September of 1948 the Presidential election campaign was under way. On September 24 President and Mrs. Truman and their daughter, Margaret, arrived in San Diego by train. Eileen was there to greet them, along with the rest of the press. In an article that came out that day, Eileen wrote:

> Mrs. Truman received visitors at an early hour reception today in her private car. Like Mrs.

> Roosevelt, she is not photogenic and those who are prepared to meet them through photographs are pleasantly surprised. Mrs. Truman is 63 and looks younger; she's plump and admits, like most mature American women, that she worries about her weight. Her softly curled hair is gray and her blue eyes reflect kindness.
>
> … [She] is essentially a small town woman, and not ashamed of it, and 20 years in the public spotlight hasn't changed her, according to Missouri friends.

Margaret particularly impressed Eileen. Eileen wrote of her:

> She has a friendly and natural charm … She's a good-natured traveler and one of the best campaigners in the family … There is an attractive mother-daughter relationship between Mrs. Truman and Margaret. Margaret tends to protect her mother from those who would deprive her of a reasonable amount of privacy.

As for President Truman, Eileen did not write about him—her assignments only involved women—but she told her friends that he had the brightest eyes and the freshest complexion of any man she had ever seen. She said he looked years younger than his actual age.

*

In the summer preceding the Trumans' visit, Eileen had interviewed the great coloratura soprano Amelita Galli-Curci. Madame Galli-Curci was making plans to live in the San Diego area. Eileen was glad that once again San Diego was attracting national and international figures. Well-known people were turning up in town just as they had before the war. Conditioned now to the appearance in San Diego of people with famous names, Eileen was ready for the phone call she received one night in late December.

I was giving a holiday party in the studio that evening for some of my college-age friends. Our group was to continue on to a dinner dance after my party. Just as the guests began to arrive, Eileen answered the phone and heard a man's voice say, "Is this Eileen Jackson?"

When she replied in the affirmative, the man informed her that he was Senator John Bricker's son, that he was in San Diego for a day or two, and that Eileen's congressman had told him to call Eileen when he got to town.

Feeling in an expansive mood, Eileen invited Senator Bricker's son to come on out to the house. "My daughter's giving a party tonight for her young friends," she said, "and I know she would like to have you join us."

Eileen had never met Senator John Bricker of Ohio, but she had certainly heard of him. He was well known both as a U.S. senator and as the Republican Vice Presidential candidate in 1944. She had never met his son, either, but she was sure that the younger Bricker would fit in with my guests. When she discovered that Mr. Bricker was staying downtown, at the Grant Hotel, on San Diego's central plaza, her mood grew even more expansive. She added, "My husband will drive down and pick you up outside the hotel. He'll be there in fifteen minutes. He would love to do that!"

Everett was surprised when informed of his assignment. He wasn't at all sure that "he would love to do that," but Eileen had promised Senator Bricker's son a ride, so off Everett went.

As soon as the man looked into Everett's car window, and expressed his pleasure at being invited out to the house, Everett knew that this was *not* Senator Bricker's son. Everett felt sure that this man was not staying at the Grant Hotel. He was clearly a tramp, or close to it, and definitely a weirdo. In 1948 people were less fearful of strangers than they are today, even of weird strangers. Nowadays, upon meeting such a person, one would roll up the window and drive away *fast*. But in 1948 Everett thought it would be fun to take this impostor home, to teach Eileen not to be so hospitable to strangers in the future.

When the two arrived at our house, everyone, including

Eileen, could see that "Mr. Bricker" was a fraud. My friends were amused by the situation, and they crowded around the grungy newcomer to ask him questions. He, meanwhile, was having a great time eating the hors d'oeuvres and drinking the liquor my parents had provided. He was happy and very much at ease until some of the questions my friends were asking began to annoy him. Then he started to crack.

When one young man, who was familiar with Washington, D.C., asked "Mr. Bricker" where his family lived in the capital, the stranger snarled, "Trying to trap me, huh? Trying to trap me!"

At that, Everett decided that Eileen's invitee had stayed long enough, that it was time for him to return to the plaza. "Mr. Bricker" protested that he was having fun and wanted to remain at the party, but Everett was firm with him. For the ride downtown, Everett showed more caution than he had earlier. He enlisted two of my male guests to go with him and "Mr. Bricker." Everett first chose a slender young man who was an artist, and then, exhibiting still more caution, he asked a new boyfriend of mine to join them. My new friend was six feet three and a half inches tall and a member of the Yale wrestling team.

After that, the party got even funnier. It happened that that same evening a truly distinguished person was staying in the apartment downstairs. The current renters were two single women—divorcees or widows, I forget which—and one was named Virginia Hoffman Wood. Her brother, Paul Hoffman, was visiting her that night. Paul Hoffman was head of the ECA (the Economic Cooperation Administration). The ECA administered the European Recovery Program, which was better known as the Marshall Plan. That meant that Paul Hoffman was in charge of running the famous Marshall Plan.

Before Everett left with "Mr. Bricker" and the bodyguards, he sneaked downstairs and told Virginia Wood and her brother about the mysterious oddball whom Eileen had invited to our house.

After Everett and his companions were gone, the phone rang again. When Eileen answered it, a man's voice said, "Is this Eileen Jackson? Well, I'm Senator Fulbright's son, and

Margaret Truman told me to get in touch with you if I ever came to San Diego."

My mother laughed and said, "Paul Hoffman, I know your voice! You come up here right now!"

Paul Hoffman joined our party, and Eileen introduced him to the assembled guests. "This is Paul Hoffman," she announced proudly. "He heads the Marshall Plan, you know."

"Oh, yeah?" said one of my friends. "Now, Mrs. Jackson, do you honestly think we'll believe that's Paul Hoffman?"

Several days later, after doing some checking, Eileen learned that "Senator Bricker's son" made a habit of going from city to city and calling the society editors of newspapers. He would assume a famous name and hope that his new identity would get him a good meal or a place to stay for the night. The police said he was a nuisance, but harmless. Everett thought "Mr. Bricker" would have achieved more success as a moocher and charlatan if he had dressed better.

*

In the spring of 1949 Eileen's mother died. Eileen had always been close to both her parents. She had written them almost daily from Mexico in the 1920s, partly because the writer in her needed an outlet, but also because she wanted to share her experiences with them. She felt especially close to her mother, who, she said, was her best friend.

Eileen's mother, a woman of no social pretensions whatsoever, had married at eighteen. Her health was poor for much of her life, but she possessed an indomitable spirit. In the late 1930s she blossomed. Living in the little country town of Lakeside, twenty-two miles northeast of San Diego, she joined the Lakeside Women's Club in order to meet some of her fellow townswomen. To her family's surprise, she soon became president of the club. She went on to become president of the San Diego County Federation of Women's Clubs, and after that, first vice president of the Southern District of the California Federation. The only thing that kept her from rising further as a clubwoman was a major illness—this time a heart attack suffered by my grandfather. She dropped her club work to care for him, and then became ill again herself. She was just sixty-two when she died. During the early years of the forties, the *Union* often featured large pictures of her on the club page of its society section, one page over from Eileen's "Tete-a-Tete" column. Eileen was proud of her mother's late-blooming talent for leadership, and in 1949 she was heartbroken to lose her greatest supporter and closest friend.

For some months prior to my grandmother's death, she and my grandfather had been living with my parents and me. Afterwards my grandfather continued to live with us. He was a droll, sweet-natured man, the pet of everyone who knew him.

*

Later that same spring Eileen and Everett decided they should go back and visit their honeymoon town of Chapala. They asked Lowell Houser if he would like to go with them. He told them, "Yes, indeed!" This would be the first long trip any of them had taken since the twenties. The three made plans to leave in July, and they began their preparations.

When Eileen and Everett went to obtain their tourist cards for entry into mainland Mexico, the Mexican official gave them forms to fill out and then asked Eileen if she had any identifying scars on her body.

"Oh, yes," she said. She pointed out her scarred leg, and showed the man a scar on her arm, left over from the time the automobile had hit her. "Here's another on my arm," she continued, "and one on my finger, and one on my hand, and one..."

"That's enough, Eileen," said Everett. He knew that she had sat down on a broken beer bottle as a child, and he saw no reason for her to mention, or to point out, the scar that had resulted from *that* accident.

"And you, *señor*," said the official, "do you have any identifying scars?"

"Not one!" Everett replied.

Eileen, Everett, and Lowell spent a busy week in Chapala.

They revisited the places they had loved twenty-three years before, and they renewed old friendships. After they left Chapala, they traveled by bus to the romantic mining town of Guanajuato. Eileen wrote five articles for the *Journal* about their experiences in Mexico that July.

When Lowell and my parents had been home just a few weeks, they took off again for Mexico. This time they went on a camping trip to Baja California. My wrestler boyfriend and I joined them. In an editorial entitled "A Day and a World Away" Eileen wrote about our camp:

> We're in a rut and it's a deep one in any rugged Mexican road. We sought it again last week when given the opportunity to leave the desk for a week. It led us to Punta San Isidro, 14 dusty ungraded miles west to the picturesque coast from the stop in the road called San Vicente … in Lower California.
>
> We pitched our pup tents on a bluff overlooking our private cove. Sentinels over this particular seashore paradise were hundreds of professorial pelicans which had painted their rock island as white as the foam that lapped at it. A sea lion barked at us every day before dawn.
>
> Those in our camp lived off the land and the sea for seven days, broiling lobsters trapped in the kelp beds two miles south of our cove, cooking fresh corn with green peppers which grow side by side in nearby Mexican fields, boiling pismo clams which reveal themselves when the tide is out on a wonderful long beach to the north, pounding abalone which also flourish here the way they used to in La Jolla …
>
> We made friends with a lobster trapper's family which lives in a tiny adobe house on the bleak bluff. The casa was spotless inside despite its dirt floor. In one corner presided a tiny cook stove, the kind artist Thomas Benton liked to paint. On it always was a big tin can filled with boiling water for the

> lobsters, and hugging it in the cool of the evening was a barrel filled with chirping chicks which would soon be big enough to join the fenceless brood outside. At "cocktail hour" the senora served us coffee and cake made without milk. The next day we shared our canned milk supply with her and her gratitude was extravagant.
>
> Another night we were invited to dine with the Mexican who presided at the village pump, and his family, and were served chicken and rice steamed in chicken broth by lamp light in a stark white and cozy kitchen. Later we sat in stiff red velvet chairs in the bedroom which also served as the sitting room and talked in limited Spanish on everything from American commercials on the radio programs to the floods that sometimes come down the San Vicente wash.
>
> It was a good camp and one of many moods, created by the light fog which sifted in each day from the sea to veil the barren brown landscape with a moor-like mystery.
>
> It is only a day and world away from a San Diego desk, and in our opinion the best possible escape. After a week there the urbanite returns, tanned, dirty, sand-flea bitten but refreshed.

*

On May 27, 1950, the *Journal* folded. It came crashing down, to almost everyone's surprise. Even though Eileen had known that the paper was having problems, she was shocked when the collapse occurred.

The Union-Tribune Publishing Company acquired the *Journal*'s "name and good will," and the *Tribune* hired several of the *Journal*'s reporters and editors, including Neil Morgan. But no one offered to hire Eileen. Rumor had it that the Copley Press hierarchy considered her to have been "disloyal" when she left the *Union*; the word was that she would never work for the

Copley Press again.

This was all particularly ironic, for in the June 1950 issue of *San Diego Magazine* Eileen was named one of the six "most powerful" (meaning influential) women in the community. When the article was written, Eileen was still the society editor of the *Journal*. By the time the article was published, however, she was a newspaperless newspaperwoman—a woman, as she said with a rueful laugh, who could exert no influence at all.

I was away at college when the *Journal* folded. In a letter written to me on May 28, 1950, Eileen described the days leading up to that traumatic event. She wrote:

> The Journal closed its doors Friday, and Monday for the first time since you were 1 year old I do not go to work. The thing came, finally, with overwhelming finality and oddly enough as a shock, because we had been conditioned for so many months to the fact that a failing paper does drag on. Someday I will tell you in detail about the dramatic last day—how I went on making up the pages with long-faced printers around me. Then we learned that the next day, Saturday, there would appear in the paper an advertisement telling that the Union-Tribune had taken over our circulation and our national syndicates. Still only rumor, but when I left for the ball I was sure we had failed—but decided to go on with colors flying anyway. I went on television that night as society editor of the Journal, knowing there was no Journal—wearing my "social scene" headdress, which was fabulous ... I won a prize, needless to say.
>
> Well, what now? The telephone has been ringing madly day and night, with honest well-wishers, with curiosity seekers ... and friends, wondering what I am going to do now, wondering if I am sorry I ever left the Union, advising me to rest, to write a book, etc.
>
> Mr. Kennedy called just before the paper came

> out announcing the folding. My first official word from a higher-up. However, I am glad I was not told because then I could be honest with the dozens of other stricken employees who asked me, as a so-called executive, what I thought. If I had known I would have felt like a heel lying to them. He was very nice, very solemn, and I was very cordial, told him I was pleased they [the Kennedys] were staying as they were genuinely popular.

Mr. and Mrs. Kennedy did stay in town. They had made many friends in San Diego since their arrival two and a half years before, and no one wanted to see them go. Mr. Kennedy continued to play a part in the city's development, dropping the newspaper business for TV. They both remained close friends of my parents, as did Mr. Kennedy's general manager, Howard Chernoff, and his wife, Melva.

On May 31, 1950, a small local paper called the *Greater La Mesa News* printed an article about Eileen. In it the writer expressed admiration for her as she faced the dissolution of the *Journal*. The article was entitled "A Salute to Eileen Jackson," and it said:

> "Noblesse oblige" was never more staunchly illustrated than by Eileen Jackson at the Masked Headdress Ball at Hotel del Coronado Friday night.
>
> For almost a quarter of a century, Eileen has recorded the social scene in San Diego. Of all the stories she wrote, and of all those she heard but could not write, about social dilemmas and obligations, none was more poignant than her own Friday night.
>
> Although she had not yet been officially notified that the *Journal*, of which she was society editor, would cease publication the next day, Eileen had a pretty good idea that the announcement would be made within a matter of hours.

But Eileen, like the other society editors, had plugged the ball to benefit the Damon Runyon cancer fund. One of the highlights of the ball was the presentation of prizes for best headdresses. One class of competition was that of society editors.

To stay away from the party would be letting down her hostess, spoiling to some extent the elaborately planned benefit.

So Eileen lived up to her social obligations, [and] went to the ball wearing the headdress … created by her artist husband.

That the headdress was so clever that it took first prize only added to the strain. All the time Eileen stood in front of the television camera and smiled, the words "society editor of the *San Diego Journal*" must have been flaying her spirit.

Chief conversation piece at the ball was the rumored collapse of the *Journal*. A good deal of the talk must have centered about Eileen and her probable future. Yet through it all, she kept her head high, her smile bright.

In spectacular fashion, Eileen Jackson lived up to the society obligations of which she had so often written.

Eileen's parents, Edward and Vera Dwyer, at the time of their wedding, 1905

Eileen as a baby, 1906

Eileen with her mother and her brother, Bill, 1907

Bill and Eileen in Ramona, 1918

Eileen as a senior at San Diego High School, 1923 (next page)

RTSOOK
PHOTO

Eileen in Chapala, Mexico, September 1926. She is wearing her wedding dress

Everett in Mexico City, December 25, 1926

Eileen and Everett's honeymoon villa, El Manglar, on the shores of Lake Chapala, Mexico, 1926 (next page)

Eileen on her first camping trip, in Texas, 1927 (next page)

Eileen standing in front of the Hunters' Den, near Palestine, Texas, 1927 (next page)

Portrait of Eileen painted by Everett in 1927

Eileen in the 1930s in San Diego (next page)

Eileen holding me in San Diego, March 1930

Eileen at the House of the Coyote's Song, 1948 (next page)

Poster exhibited on San Diego streetcars and buses in 1948, announcing Eileen's move to the *Journal*

Pat Nixon and Eileen at their first meeting, May 1956 (next page)

Eileen on the phone, her file cards in front of her, early 1960s (next page)
photograph courtesy of the San Diego Historical Society

Everett in the studio at the House of the Coyote's Song, 1963 (following page)

Eileen in the mid-1960s (previous page)

Everett and Eileen in Mexico City at the opening of Everett's retrospective exhibition, 1979

Eileen, Everett, and Betty Hubbard at Eileen's eightieth birthday party, 1986

Eileen in the garden at the House of the Coyote's Song, early 1990s (following page)

Battling Leisure

In its August 1950 issue, *San Diego Magazine* printed an article by Eileen on the subject of leisure. It was called "Living In Leisure and Not Liking It." It was illustrated with a photo of Eileen wearing her prize-winning headdress, the one Everett had created for her for the Headdress Ball.

In the article Eileen made it clear that a life of leisure was not for her. No longer did she praise leisure, the way she had praised it in her editorial about camping at Laguna Hanson. No longer was she charmed by "days exquisitely wasted." She explained that she was stunned when the *Journal* folded, and she said she missed the women she used to call each week. She wanted to describe their dresses again, and to chase after them at parties and balls, with a cameraman in tow. She wanted, in other words, to go back to work! Eileen was reacting poorly to her forced "retirement."

Actually, by the time the August edition of *San Diego Magazine* came out, she had already found a new job. On July 11, 1950, a weekly called *The Chronicle* made its debut in San Diego. It was a nonpartisan paper devoted to local news, and Eileen was its Women's Page editor. The publisher sent the first four issues as samples to over ninety thousand San Diego County homes. After that, the people in those homes were supposed to start subscribing. Several of Eileen's staff members at the *Journal* had joined her on this new little paper, and they helped her fill the social section of *The Chronicle* with news.

Unfortunately, the paper folded after only four months. But Eileen wrote some entertaining articles for *The Chronicle* before it went under. She interviewed New York City's former Mayor William O'Dwyer, who was visiting California on his way to his post as U.S. ambassador to Mexico; she wrote two feature articles on the Prince of Wales's visit to Coronado in 1920; and she produced some more lively social editorials. Her last editorial in *The Chronicle*, written when she knew the paper was about to fold, was entitled "This is Getting to be a Habit."

Eileen may have ended her career on that paper with humor, but she began it with a bombshell. Her July 11, 1950, editorial in *The Chronicle* deserves special mention, for it was an amazing one. It could have been written today by the most ardent feminist. In 1950 Eileen had no pressing financial obligations. During her period of enforced idleness she must have realized, all rationalizations aside, why she *really* wanted to work. Never before had she made such an unequivocal statement regarding women and the home. Although she had come close in her wartime editorial "Leading Double Lives," her comments in that editorial were mild compared to the ones in this latest piece. To my knowledge she never again spoke out so defiantly. But her actions from 1950 on would prove that she meant what she said when she wrote the following editorial:

> A woman's place is not in the home.
>
> This we know for sure now that we have been relegated to it for a few weeks after being a career woman for nearly 22 consecutive years. We know we are not apt to offend young men and women with this statement which is a denial of tradition, but we probably will invite the opposition of their parents.
>
> Where is her place, then? If she is healthy, not lazy and fairly intelligent it should be where she can express herself as an individual, lifting herself from the role of a docile dependent which neither she nor her family respects.
>
> What about her children, and her husband? We're thinking about them when we insist that she should be given scope to contribute her share not

only to the home but to the stimulating world outside. Then when she, as a complete, unfettered individual, touches their lives she brings home something vital, infectious in its force, to them.

We don't mean she should necessarily have a job although we would recommend it when her children are out of the nursery. It could be a volunteer or a part-time job which would acquaint her with community projects and make her socially responsible. It might be a job with a salary which would help her husband who needs it in these days of soaring living costs. There's nothing like a paycheck for morale-lifting independence and a sense of personal dignity.

The "job" might be a creative career in the fields of art, music, drama or literature, even on an amateur basis. But a job or outside interests she needs.

A dozen years ago Pearl Buck wrote a controversial article on what she called "America's Medieval Women." She blamed the men for contributing their part to women's home enslavement through their traditional male pride in not wanting them to work.

She pointed out that American women were educated to work and trained for equality in a modern school system and then forced into a prison cell which offered no outlet for their skilled energies.

She insisted that it is not only wasteful but dangerous to educate women as we do for our present state of traditionalism. It's like putting new wine into old bottles. Miss Buck held, as do we, that there is more to life than a limited home front, for a woman must feel herself growing and becoming more and more complete as an individual.

Miss Buck asked more than a decade ago:

"When will American men learn that they cannot expect happiness with a woman who is not her whole self?"

Since that day when she accused America of being backward in its attitude toward women, of morally shutting the door on them and of suggesting that home ought to be enough for a nice woman, the outlook has brightened.

We think she would be heartened if she could observe the attitude of the young college men and women today. A man, one of our contemporaries, denied his wife the right to get a job because it reflected on his ability to support her. His son frankly suggested that his bride work along with him until they are able to start a family.

The young man admitted that if she were expected to help with the income he should share the home responsibilities, and he agreed foresightedly that his wife should not be curbed from returning to outside interests after the family had been safely launched.

A woman's place is in the world. We admit it is a good world when it revolves around the home, but the orbit should be wide.

*

For a year and a half after *The Chronicle* folded, Eileen did not work on a newspaper. She managed to stay active, however. During that period she wrote a few articles for *San Diego Magazine*, and she found other ways to keep busy. In the summer of 1950, from August 1 through September 9, San Diego staged a celebration that commemorated California's century of statehood. After the festival was over, the president of the San Diego City and County Centennial Commission, a business and civic leader named George A. Scott, hired Eileen to write a lengthy, detailed report on San Diego's portion of the centennial celebration. Her report is now on file in the San Diego Public Library. Perhaps some committee in the year 2050 will dig it out and study it when California celebrates two hundred years as a state.

The centennial project kept Eileen occupied for several months, and during that time she also helped put on a wedding. In the winter of 1951 I married Duncan Waterman, the young man from Yale. Ours was the second wedding held in the studio. Eileen led a leisurely life from then until September, when she became public relations director and membership chairman of the YWCA.

She worked at the Y for less than a year, but in that short while she made a strong impression on the staff. With her usual creative flair, she came up with ideas to increase membership. Her most famous effort involved the figure-control classes at the Y. Eileen had a brilliant idea on how to publicize them. Her friend Michele (Mickey) Miller helped her with this project. Mickey, who a year later would become the third bride to be married in the studio, had worked with Eileen on both the *Journal* and *The Chronicle*. By the time the figure-control classes opened, in October of 1951, Mickey was writing for the *Tribune*. Eileen persuaded her to take one of the four-week classes, and to report her weight-loss progress in the *Tribune*.

Mickey has never seemed even remotely overweight to me, but she says that at that point in her life she thought a few less pounds on her frame would do her good. Her introductory article, entitled "Hip, Hips Away," appeared on September 24, and for the next four weeks she wrote two stories a week about the class. A different photo of her accompanied her story each time, and each time in the photo she looked slimmer.

Mickey's articles sparkled, and her progress was impressive. In four weeks she lost not only ten pounds but also several inches from her hips, waist, and calves. In her articles she gave the figure-control class full credit for her gradually changing silhouette. Women began to take an interest in Mickey's weight loss, and soon many had joined the Y and signed up for the class. In a story about the Y that Eileen wrote for *San Diego Magazine* in 1952, she reported that by the end of October 1951 "there were nearly 650 women in the figure control classes alone at the YW."

*

In the fall of 1951, after she had helped launch the figure-control classes, Eileen took some time off from her Y work. She flew back to Columbia, South Carolina, for a brief visit, to care for me and my new baby. During her absence Everett painted a large mural on a wall of the upstairs kitchen. In it he depicted the YWCA building. Anyone could see that a figure-control class was going on inside, for a different-sized woman was standing in each window of the Y. Next to the building he drew a street filled with people, and he painted a banner on the Y's roof that said, "Welcome Home, Eileen!" The mural was ready to greet Eileen when she returned from South Carolina.

Toward the end of Eileen's stay in Columbia, she expressed an interest in visiting the seaport city of Charleston. After I had assured her that her new grandson and I would be all right without her, she flew to Charleston for the day. While she was there she had a lovely experience, one that she talked about for years afterwards.

She arrived in Charleston and decided to eat a quick lunch before exploring the city. She chose a nice-looking restaurant that turned out to be a popular one. Upon entering it, she discovered that it was packed with women diners; there were no tables free. She was about to leave when the manager came up to her and told her that an elderly lady at one of the tables had noticed her. The manager said the woman would like Eileen to join her, if Eileen didn't mind sitting with a stranger.

Eileen was happy to join the older woman. She sat down, and soon the two were carrying on a conversation as though they had known each other all their lives. When the lady discovered that Eileen could spend only a few hours in Charleston before flying back to Columbia, she insisted on becoming her tour guide. In her chauffeur-driven car, she showed Eileen the sights of Charleston. She pointed out various historic buildings, and she had the driver stop several times along their route, so she and Eileen could get out and enter some of the buildings. Hearing that Eileen wanted to buy a set of pewter candlesticks, she took her to an antique shop. Eileen said that all of the shop personnel expressed delight at seeing the little old lady, and they greeted her by name. She was obviously a woman of importance in Charleston.

When the tour was over, she insisted that Eileen come and see her house. It turned out to be an old, beautifully furnished Charleston mansion. After showing Eileen through the house, her hostess led her into a peaceful walled garden. As they sat down in that leafy, tranquil garden, a servant brought them tea. After a while the lady had her chauffeur drive them both to the airport, where she and Eileen said good-bye.

Eileen felt that she had stepped into another world that day. When she returned to Columbia, she told Duncan and me that she would never forget the hours she spent in Charleston, or her gracious Charleston guide.

*

In the spring of 1952 Eileen helped promote a benefit baseball game for the Y. The game, which took place on May 8, featured the San Diego Padres, of the old Pacific Coast League. They played the Sacramento Solons that night and won. The YWCA had bought out the field for the night, and had had no trouble disposing of the tickets. The event was a sellout because Eileen and a large volunteer committee of Y members and community leaders had persuaded every socialite in town to attend the game. Art Linkletter was the master of ceremonies that evening. The benefit ended up making a net profit of $12,154, which went to the Y's remodeling fund. Since that ball game was Eileen's final project at the Y, she was elated that it had brought in so much money.

*

That spring the *Union* rehired Eileen. On May 16, 1952, just eight days after the ball game, her new column appeared in the paper. It was called "Straws in the Wind."

The summer that followed that spring was memorable for everyone at the House of the Coyote's Song. My little son and I spent three months there as we prepared to join Duncan at his Army post in Panama. Eileen was happy to be a newspaperwoman again. The parties she covered were becoming more frequent and more glamorous, but the pace of her life had not yet reached frenzied proportions. She still spent many evenings at home. On those occasions our family would barbecue in the upper patio of the house. While we were standing beside the grill, we would wave at the tenants, Gene and Betty Peach, who were barbecuing in their patio below. We would also hover around the new television set at night, to watch in wide-eyed fascination the 1952 political conventions. Occasionally the Peaches hovered with us. They were both newspaper reporters, but, like their fellow reporter Eileen, they were not above slumming once in a while by watching TV.

Max and Margaret Miller often came by that summer, as did Lowell Houser and some new friends of my parents: Bob and LaRue Thompson, Ray and Irma Stoudt, George Phillips, the world's foremost authority on chimney sweeps. All those people are gone now—the Thompsons, Stoudts, Millers, George and Lowell—but they were vivid presences in our patio that summer. In varying combinations, we would sit out there and talk.

My baby son was also present in the patio. He created his own little world in his playpen, with my grandfather in constant attendance. Everyone agreed later that it was a special time. It was a time when we all seemed to pause for a minute and catch our breath, even our leisure-hater, Eileen. It was the summer that we always referred to afterwards as "that summer when everybody was so happy—that golden summer of '52."

*

Many exciting things happened to Eileen during the next few years. Her career took off in a dazzling fashion. She attended more parties than she had ever attended in her life, and she wrote them up in long columns of vivid, descriptive prose. She wrote a short piece on Eddie Cantor in 1952 (he was one of the few men she ever interviewed); she interviewed Queen Frederika of Greece in Los Angeles in 1953; and in 1954 she again went to Los Angeles, to interview Madame Bayar, the wife of the President of Turkey. That same year, she traveled with Everett to Guatemala, Honduras, and southern Mexico, and wrote articles for the *Union* about their trip. Also in 1954 she interviewed two impressive women from Spain: Madame de Lequerica, the wife of Spain's ambassador to the United States, and Señora Maria Luisa Caturla, the famed Spanish art historian. Eileen and Everett entertained Señora Caturla one afternoon in the studio.

Everett, too, was busy during those years. Besides painting, taking trips, and going to parties, he was also illustrating books. He had illustrated one book before the war, Max Miller's *Mexico Around Me*, which was published in 1937. Then in 1944 he began illustrating books for the Limited Editions Club and the Heritage Press. His publisher was a man named George Macy. Mr. Macy was a great admirer of Everett *and* his art. The affection and admiration were mutual. As Everett said, he and George Macy were "on the same wave length."

The first book Everett illustrated for Mr. Macy was *The Wonderful Adventures of Paul Bunyan*, as retold by the poet and anthologist Louis Untermeyer. In 1956 the Macys and the Untermeyers visited San Diego, and Eileen and Everett gave a dinner party for them in the studio.

In a letter Eileen wrote to Duncan and me, she indicated that it was quite an evening. Included at the party were two close friends of Eileen and Everett's—the beautiful, glamorous Jo Bobbie MacConnell and her quiet but debonair husband, Mac. Jo Bobbie was a war widow with a small son when she married Mac, who was twenty years her senior. When the MacConnells were not traveling, they lived in a dramatic house perched just above the ocean, in the little town of La Jolla, the upscale beach community thirteen miles north of San Diego.

Jo Bobbie is bright as well as beautiful. Eileen felt that she and Mac would not only add glamor to the evening but would also contribute brains and sophistication. As might be expected, the dinner-table discussion that night revolved around art and poetry. Eileen told her guests the story of her meeting the poet Carl Sandburg when she was a cub reporter on the *Sun*. Eileen said that the college textbook that contained Mr. Sandburg's poem "Grass" was an anthology compiled by Louis Untermeyer.

After that, the group began to discuss other poets. Jo Bobbie mentioned that she had read a work of prose by the poet Sara Teasdale.

"Sara Teasdale never wrote any prose," said Mr. Untermeyer.

"Oh, but she did!" said Jo Bobbie.

"No, she didn't!" insisted Louis Untermeyer.

The argument continued until Mr. Untermeyer attempted to settle it once and for all.

"I ought to know!" he exclaimed. "I used to sleep with her!"

That stopped the conversation for a moment, Eileen reported, but then Jo Bobbie ran to the phone and called her son at home. She told him where to find her copy of Sara Teasdale's prose, and to read some of it over the phone to Mr. Untermeyer. That point having been proved at last, the party went on. It was, as Eileen said, quite an evening.

Everett liked Louis Untermeyer very much. In a letter to Duncan and me in which he described that dinner party, Everett told us that he found Mr. Untermeyer to be a "very kind, very sympathetic, very brilliant man." That night Louis Untermeyer signed Everett's copy of *Paul Bunyan* and wrote: "To the *real* artist, EGJ, from the mere reteller."

Everett also liked Mrs. Untermeyer. In his letter Everett said that one San Diegan who met her described her as "ill-natured," that another described her as "disagreeable," and that even Eileen found her "questionable." But Everett said he thought she was "adorable."

In that same letter to Duncan and me, Everett added that he and Eileen had recently made two new friends, whom he knew Duncan and I would like. They were Ted and Helen Geisel. Ted was better known as Dr. Seuss. Everett wrote, "If I find many more such people, I might actually not want to retire to Honduras when the time comes."

Washington, D.C. and San Francisco

On Eileen's fiftieth birthday, in 1956, Everett wrote my family a letter in which he said:

> This is Eileen's birthday. Fifty years ago she began life on this earth very tightly wound. I have known her now some thirty years but have not by any means explored her completely. She remains physically charming having today the figure of a maiden, and her zest for humanity is undiminished.
>
> The factor thing which gives meaning and full justification to existence to her is people. Hers is a world of people and she would be the last one to volunteer for a trial run to the moon. She loves people. Indeed she loves all people, and each and every individual is for her a devoted friend until he proves otherwise. But of them all, those she loves most are the members of her family, and it is for them that she lives. Today is her birthday, and I salute her for a thousand reasons, and especially for being a completely UNselfcentered celebrity in her own community.

In 1956 Eileen's paper gave her the opportunity to associate with more people than usual, and I made it possible for her to demonstrate, yet again, her devotion to the members of her family.

Early in 1956 Eileen's editor asked her if she would like to cover the Republican political convention in San Francisco that

August. She said yes, she would like to very much. She of course would be writing about the wives of the politicians, not about the politicians themselves, but that was fine with her. In late April she was looking ahead to her summertime assignment, and was trying to do her homework regarding some of the women she would meet at the convention, when suddenly I became very ill. By then Duncan and our two little boys and I were living in Virginia just outside Washington, D.C. Eileen dropped everything and flew back to take care of her grandchildren while I was in the hospital. Everett and my grandfather remained at home. They were occupying the whole house at that point, for my parents had finally stopped renting the lower two floors.

Eileen managed very well in Virginia, although the boys almost put one over on her when they filled the bathtub with bath toys, climbed into the water together, and then insisted that "Mommie always lets us take the tricycle into the tub!"

When I got out of the hospital and began to feel stronger, Eileen checked in with the paper. Her editor told her that he wanted her to interview several women in Washington before she came home.

I like to think my illness served a useful purpose, for it caused Eileen to meet a woman that spring whom she would count forever after as a friend—not a close friend, but definitely a friend. Why one person is especially drawn to another after only a few seconds is hard to explain, but instant affinities do occur. Eileen often clicked with people in that way. The little old lady in Charleston and Eileen were immediately drawn to each other, as were Ellis Spreckels and Eileen. The same can be said about Pat Nixon and my mother.

Eileen's editor wanted her to interview Mrs. Thomas Kuchel, Mrs. Charles Thomas, Mrs. Richard Nixon, and Mrs. Mary Jane McCaffree. He chose those four women because three of them had ties to California and one had a tie to the nation's First Lady, Mamie Eisenhower. Mrs. Kuchel's husband was a U.S. senator from California, Mrs. Thomas was a Californian whose husband was Secretary of the Navy, Mrs. Nixon was also a Californian and the wife of the Vice President of the United States, and Mrs. McCaffree was Mamie Eisenhower's social secretary. The Washington bureau of the Copley Press would set up the interviews and provide a photographer to take pictures.

Eileen visited Mrs. Kuchel in her Washington apartment. The article Eileen wrote about the visit began, "The senator's wife with the mispronounced name and the pronounced beauty is Mrs. Thomas Kuchel of California." Eileen interviewed Mrs. Thomas in her apartment, too, and they discussed Washington protocol in some detail and Mrs. Thomas' own busy social schedule.

Eileen's interview with Mary Jane McCaffree took place on a rainy May afternoon in what Eileen described as "the comparatively drab east entrance of the White House." A guard let her in, and an attendant showed her what to do. In the article Eileen wrote for the paper, she said:

> We were asked first to scan big black books filled with clippings of articles on the first lady. We assumed we were to learn from them the acceptable style of White House interviews.
>
> We digested them too soon to please the attendant, who seemed reluctant to call Mrs. McCaffree. We had heard she was as inaccessible as Mrs. Eisenhower, who understandably has not the time or energy for private interviews.
>
> As a result we were not prepared for Mrs. McCaffree's relaxed graciousness and generosity, which permitted us to satisfy our curiosity about Mrs. Eisenhower for more than an hour.

Eileen went on to describe Mrs. Eisenhower's appearance and personality traits as seen through the eyes of her social secretary.

Those three interviews were easy to set up, but the interview with Mrs. Nixon presented a problem. Mrs. Nixon did not like being interviewed. She was a busy woman, with two young daughters to rear, and she was wary of the press.

As a result, Eileen only got as far as the Vice President on her first try. When she met Vice President Nixon, in his office in the Capitol, he told her that his wife was not giving interviews but that he would be glad to talk to Eileen in his wife's place. Eileen told him that she wrote for the Women's Page and would prefer an interview with Mrs. Nixon.

Vice President Nixon knew that the *San Diego Union* was a conservative paper, and that it would be supporting the Republican ticket that fall. That probably influenced his decision to let Eileen spend a few minutes with his wife, or perhaps, like President Roosevelt, he sensed that Eileen was a kindly person, who could never "hurt anybody." He asked his social secretary, Priscilla Joy Everts, to arrange a short meeting.

A few days later Eileen met Mrs. Nixon in a room in the Capitol. The interview was to last no longer than fifteen minutes, but the second those two met they knew they liked each other. The chemistry was instantaneous. They ended up talking for over an hour. They discovered they had things in common. They both had Irish fathers with connections to Nevada: Mrs. Nixon's father had been a miner in Nevada; Eileen's father was born in Virginia City during the silver rush. They both had honeymooned in Mexico. They couldn't stop talking. At the end of the interview, as they reluctantly said good-bye, Mrs. Nixon exclaimed, "Oh, darn! I wish I weren't so busy. I would go out and take care of your daughter when you leave, if only I didn't have so much to do!"

It was that kind of a meeting. Eileen liked all the other women she had interviewed in Washington, just as she liked the various women she had interviewed in California over the years, but she came away from her meeting with Pat Nixon feeling that she had found a friend.

Eileen wrote an article about Mrs. Nixon that captured the spirit of the interview. Later, at the Republican convention in August, Vice President Nixon told Eileen that he thought her article was the best one ever written about his wife. The photographer took a picture of the two new friends the day they met. They are pictured sitting on a couch together. The *Union* ran the photo to illustrate the story. On June 12 Eileen received a note from Mrs. Nixon in which she wrote:

> This is just a note to tell you how much I enjoyed our visit when you were in Washington recently. It was a pleasure to sit down and chat informally with a friend from home.
>
> I want to thank you too for sending me two of the articles you wrote during the time you were here. You were more than kind to say so many nice things about me, and they were deeply appreciated.
>
> I do hope the news from your daughter has been encouraging. It is hard to believe that you are a grandmother!

In August of 1956, three months after Eileen's Washington-Virginia visit, she and Everett took off for San Francisco, so that Eileen could cover the Republican national convention. Her Washington interviews had given her confidence. She felt certain she could handle this next assignment, the biggest and most important of her career.

*

Eileen had the time of her life at the Republican convention of 1956. She was in her element. During that week she competed with some of the best newswomen in the country, and she was happy to discover that she could hold her own with them. Now this, she thought, is what journalism is all about!

There were plenty of women present to offer her competition. She wrote in one of her articles:

> There were so many society editors from across the nation covering the reception given today in the Mark Hopkins Hotel by Mrs. Leonard W. Hall, wife of the Republican national chairman, for Mrs. Richard Nixon—and they were so glamorously dressed—that photographers found themselves taking pictures of scribes … It was a field day for adjective scribblers.

Eileen caught the attention of Betty Beale, social reporter on the Washington, D.C., paper *The Washington Evening Star*. Again an instantaneous friendship sprang up. Betty was tough and knowledgeable, but, like Eileen, she was the kind of person who fit in with the social set of her city. She was a hard-driving reporter and a refined, cultivated woman at the same time. She and Eileen took to each other at once.

After they knew each other better, they found that they were a lot alike. Neither dealt in gossip, and both were chided on occasion for writing columns devoid of rumor and innuendo. Neither ever took a notebook or a tape recorder to a party she was covering, and eventually both would become famous in their respective cities for attending more than three hundred parties a year. Betty would claim that one year she went to five hundred parties; Eileen would cite a more modest amount in her peak year: three hundred and twenty-five.

Also, Betty Beale was a Christian Scientist. Eileen had stopped going to the Christian Science Church after she was married, but throughout her life she held good Christian Science thoughts for her friends, often with impressive results. She even held good thoughts so that her grandson would get into medical school, although Everett pointed out that helping someone get into a medical school was probably not what Mary Baker Eddy had in mind when she taught her followers to hold those thoughts.

In 1956 Eileen had no idea that she and Betty were so similar. She just knew that she liked her and that Betty was a great friend to have at a political convention. Eileen was the novice. She let Betty guide her through the confusion and nonstop activity of the convention, and she learned as she went along. But other people helped her, too.

Perhaps Betty Beale first noticed Eileen when the two were in a room adjoining Mrs. Nixon's suite at the Mark Hopkins Hotel. They were part of a group of twenty-five reporters who were waiting to go in and interview the Vice President's wife. Mrs. Nixon asked that Eileen enter first, a courtesy that the other reporters immediately picked up on. Eileen wrote in her notes that Pat Nixon "smoothed the way for me, knowing I had never before covered the social phase of a national political convention."

During that week Eileen and Betty rushed from brunches to luncheons to teas. After a fashion-show luncheon at the Sheraton Plaza, Mamie Eisenhower stopped to shake hands and chat with a small group of reporters that included Eileen. She told them she had given them a wink from her table across from theirs at the luncheon, and Eileen reported in her column that that was true. Eileen commented on Mrs. Eisenhower's enthusiastic attitude, her pretty blue eyes, and her fresh, youthful skin.

Like Mrs. Nixon, Mary Jane McCaffree was also a help to Eileen. She of course remembered Eileen from their hour-long talk in Washington just three months before, and she was apparently as gracious in San Francisco as she had been at the White House.

In a letter Eileen wrote to Duncan and me as the convention ended, she described the excitement of the San Francisco event. One can sense her exhilaration as one reads these words:

> Dearest kids:
>
> Well—it's all wrapped up, such as it is, and was and we pull out with the VIPs tomorrow morning. It has been pressure trying to file stories by 3, and then later, and writing in a room with dozens of typewriters and two TVs going full blast. Everett has been a wonderful and sweet help ...
>
> I think my stories have been all right—I've written day and night and had lots of breaks. I saw Pat Nixon three times, met Mrs. Eisenhower, had a quickie interview, was the only woman at one of Jim Hagerty's conferences, and have hobnobbed with Mrs. William Randolph Hearst, beauteous Austine McDonnell, columnist, who sat at our press table at the luncheon for Mrs. Eisenhower. Mrs. McCaffree, social sec. to Mamie, has been particularly gracious—have met her 3 times. Believe me, my Washington interviews have served me well here—invaluable in fact. I have had

unbelievable breaks because of them. I've met and talked with them all from Mrs. George Humphrey, wife of Sec. of Treas.—was invited to walk up Nob Hill with Mrs. Brownell … Mamie shook hands with me before giving Betty Beale, the N.Y. Times, Philadelphia Inquirer, Denver Post, AP reporters and *me* an impromptu, unexpected interview. I will send all the papers when I get them.

I've hung out with Betty Beale, syndicated writer and Washington Star reporter. She's … great, outspoken … a real newshen, who took me under her wing. My paper didn't impress the big paper girls, but the gracious way I was treated by Pat Nixon, by Mary Jane McCaffree, by Sec. of Navy Thomas (he introduced me to Mrs. Charles Wilson), helped. By the end of the week I was one of the gals—we hopped from party to party like mad, nearly got thrown out of the party for Mrs. Eisenhower because we insisted on keeping a table near Mamie. Everett and I went to two champagne balls at the Civic Auditorium, I attended two breakfast briefings, fabulous affairs by Bertha Adkins, assistant to Leonard Hall, (my stories I hope were used and will be sent to you). Went to Berkeley for a big dinner … talked with Mrs. Kuchel and Mrs. Knowland. Said hello to Dorothy Thompson … Took pictures of everybody from Mrs. Sherman Adams, to Mrs. Leonard Hall—was introduced to Mrs. Stassen by Mrs. George Humphrey, none less.

The press conference with Jim Hagerty was fun. He talked at length to me and told the White House office—the one set up at the St. Francis—to be nice to me. I told him I liked his story in Time, but wondered why his hair didn't seem red. He interrupted his release on the plane, shot down by Chinese, to get me a release on Mamie. The plane story release was funny. There were present about

50 of them, TV, radio and press. He couldn't be heard very well. He announced that a plane had been lost. I thought it odd, and told the man next to me, that the White House should be so worried, adding that planes are lost every day out of a navy town like ours and the White House never takes time out to put out a bulletin on it. The reporters seemed puzzled—kept asking how many aboard, refused to believe the small number—in other words they were trying to figure out why the White House was interested. Finally when the conference was nearly over a reporter asked if there would be anything more concrete on the plane story later. Jim H. said: "All I have is that it was attacked—or believed to have been attacked." "*Attacked*!" screamed every reporter. They had not heard that all important word at first. Boy, did the pencils start to fly.

I have spent about $10 a day, sometimes $15, on taxis alone—far more than on food. I cannot evaluate how my stories seem to the public back home, but I'm glad, honestly that it is all over.

To tell the truth it's been exhilarating and once I got into the swing of it I was like an old war-horse. I had to play it by ear … Now I want to relax for months.

*

Eileen's stories went over very well with her "public back home." Her editors were so pleased with her convention coverage they decided to give her an even bigger assignment the following year. They told her they wanted her to cover the Queen of England's 1957 visit to Canada and the United States.

Following the Queen

Before Eileen left for Canada, in October of 1957, the *Union* announced to its readers:

> In a few days a gracious queen of England will arrive in Ottawa for her first visit to North America as sovereign. On the scene will be Eileen Jackson, The San Diego Union's widely informed columnist. Mrs. Jackson will report daily on the queen's visit to the United States and Canada.

Everett was going to remain in San Diego while Eileen covered the Queen's tour. This time he would be alone in the house, for my grandfather—that "truly great and good spirit," as Everett wrote of him—had died the previous March.

The minute Eileen and Everett's friends heard about Eileen's plans to follow the Queen, they began inviting Everett for dinner. Eileen hated to leave him, but he assured her that he would be well cared for by "all those women in your file," and he agreed that her new assignment was too challenging to turn down.

The night of October 9 Eileen flew to Ottawa. The next day the *Union* printed a second announcement. This one stated:

> Eileen Jackson is off to see the Queen.
>
> The writer, whose "Straws in the Wind" social column appears daily in The San Diego Union, left yesterday by air for Ottawa, Ont., Canada. She will be on hand when Queen Elizabeth and Prince Philip arrive there on Saturday.

> … Officially accredited by the White House and the Canadian and British governments for the tour, Mrs. Jackson will be a member of the huge press corps following the movements of the royal pair during the 10-day visit.
>
> A special press airlift will take Mrs. Jackson from the Canadian capital to Jamestown for the arrival of Queen Elizabeth and her husband in this country.
>
> The San Diego Union's writer's first report on the flurry of excitement in Ottawa as Canadians prepare for the visit of the Queen, will appear Friday morning.

By October 10 close to a thousand members of the media had arrived in Ottawa, although Eileen's pal Betty Beale was not among them. Betty would begin covering the Queen's tour later, in Williamsburg, Virginia.

Eileen was lonely and somewhat daunted at first, but she quickly got moving. She toured the Houses of Parliament, obtained her credentials, and received handouts at the press headquarters in the Chateau Laurier Hotel. She also found time to write Everett and describe to him the "flame-colored" fall leaves in Ottawa and the "charming, courteous Canadians." Then she began sending stories to her paper about the atmosphere in Ottawa as the city prepared to welcome Queen Elizabeth and Prince Philip.

On October 12 the royal couple arrived, and the real excitement began. That evening Eileen attended a press reception at Government House, and afterwards she filed a story to the *Union*. In it she said:

> Queen Elizabeth and Prince Philip are coming to California—not on this tour but some day.
>
> The reason I know is that I invited them and the prince accepted. He said they had been to 22 countries in the last two years and he thinks California would be a good idea.

> I reminded him that California was a state but in some ways it really was a special country …
>
> The conversation was lighthearted, but before we parted … he said, "Remember, we're coming."

Eileen's conversation with the Prince that evening caught the attention of the Associated Press, which picked up and carried the story of her invitation and the Prince's response. In her article the next day, Eileen went on to talk about Prince Philip, saying:

> Prince Philip is positively jovial and easy to meet. He walks around with his hands behind him, usually hatless. Even at the war memorial service he seemed casual, though respectful.
>
> … Prince Philip … has a teasing way. When we invited him and the queen to come to California he said it was a "great idea," adding: "We're young yet, you know, and we're used to getting around."

Eileen told her readers that she had watched the memorial service from the rooftop of the Ottawa post office. She said her companions on the roof were "some Toronto photographers who had held this strategic and precarious spot since dawn."

In that same article Eileen wrote admiringly of the Queen:

> The queen walks as if she had all the time in the world. In fact everything she does is with easy charm. When she talks to you she leads the conversation with quiet skill and you have a feeling the little tete-a-tete is as important to her as it is to you.

The next few days in Canada were busy ones for the Queen and for the reporters who followed her. Eileen was one of ten reporters who witnessed an intimate little tree-planting ceremony. In her article describing it she said:

> It was probably the most private party which

> will take place but it will be recorded around the world—50 photographers were present and only 10 reporters.
>
> We stood in a semicircle around her as she tossed a spadeful of soil onto the red maple tree roots with a four-foot silver spade. "It's a nice tree," appraised the queen. Patting the head of the Gov. Gen. Massey's golden retriever, Duff, she walked up the hill to change for the next event, the reception in our hotel, Chateau Laurier.

In a lucky draw, Eileen drew a place at that reception "on the floor" in the ballroom. She wrote Everett that she and her fellow lucky members of the reporters' pool would walk among the guests at the party while the rest of the press would be relegated to the balcony!

Eileen watched the Queen open Parliament (it was the first time a reigning monarch had opened the Canadian Parliament), and each day she described the Queen's dresses. Queen Elizabeth changed her outfits several times a day, and the press reported on each new dress as it appeared. In her notes about the trip Eileen wrote:

> … reporters were given printed releases of what the queen would wear on each occasion. In Canada sketches of the models and samples of her dress fabrics were mounted on easels to assist reporters in writing their own versions of her costumes. In Canada members of the press were told that she would not wear the same ensembles in the United States as in Canada. We were informed that she would honor Canada on Oct. 14 by wearing … to the state reception and dinner given for her … a dress which would go down in history as the "Maple Leaf of Canada" dress. On a pale green satin background a motif of Canadian maple leaves was appliquéd with crystals and simulated emeralds.

> Later when the press was given a release in Wash. D.C. that she would wear the famous "maple leaf" dress to the first state dinner, given by Pres. and Mrs. Dwight Eisenhower Oct. 17 at the White House, I was sure that a mistake had been made by those releasing her wardrobe choices. I was right and a correction was made, but not before the New York papers had released the wrong information.

At one point, while still in Canada, Eileen worked out an agreement with a male reporter on an Ottawa paper: he traded her the names of important people for the names of colors and materials to describe the Queen's clothes.

Eileen was thriving and was sending great stories home, but as she wrote Everett on one of her postcards:

> This is a rat race—never to bed before 1 A.M.—up early—so much briefing, fussing to get places, to get credentials, to be in the right place at the right time. *Believe* me it's work, and it *is* interesting, but one is on a treadmill. You leave the city newsroom (this thing is run like a big newspaper) for one minute and you miss an important announcement ...

On that same postcard Eileen promised Everett that she would "never leave home again!"

*

On October 16 Eileen flew on the press plane to Patrick Henry Airport, near Williamsburg, Virginia. She then followed the Queen and Prince as they toured nearby Jamestown and visited historic places in Williamsburg. She was happy to see Betty Beale again. Eileen had made friends with some of the reporters in Ottawa, but as she told Everett, "It is a lonely life really—everyone is fun but competitive."

On October 17 the group flew to Washington, D.C. There the Queen and Prince Philip attended a round of receptions, luncheons, and dinners. While in Washington they also took in a football game and visited a supermarket.

At a reception given at the Statler Hotel on October 17 by the Joint Committee of the Press, Radio, and Television Correspondents, Prince Philip remembered that Eileen had invited him and the Queen to visit California. A *Union* staff correspondent wrote in an article from Washington:

> Mrs. Jackson reiterated the invitation today and told him Gov. Knight had wired "me too."
>
> "Good," he replied with enthusiasm.
>
> The queen overheard and said "California?" with definite interest.

Just before the media reception at the Statler, Eileen positioned Duncan and me in the hotel lobby. She knew exactly when the royal couple would walk through the lobby. They appeared as scheduled, and our small group of spectators smiled and clapped decorously as they walked by. They smiled back at us and waved. I was overcome by Queen Elizabeth's beauty. No photo had ever done her justice. Eileen had accurately described her "sky blue eyes" and "flawless skin," and the Queen's smile was radiant.

The night of October 20 the tour moved on to New York by train. Eileen and Pat Nixon talked for a minute at the train station, before Eileen left on the press train. The next day, after a ticker-tape parade, the royal couple had lunch in the Waldorf Astoria ballroom. Eileen reported that it was "the largest (1,750 guests) and most brilliant luncheon of the tour." The royal tour continued with a white-tie banquet at the Waldorf Astoria Hotel, and ended at the Commonwealth Ball, in the armory. The Queen and Prince flew back to England that night, the Queen still wearing, as Eileen wrote in her article, "the last creation out of her fabulous tour wardrobe."

The next morning Eileen was already back in Washington, at

the Statler Hotel, preparing to interview Mrs. Thomas S. Gates, Jr., the wife of the new Secretary of the Navy.

*

Eileen had to come down gradually from her thirteen days of travel and excitement. Her idea of coming down gradually was to interview five Washington wives—some "American Queens," as she called them. Actually it was her editor's idea that she finish her trip in that way. He knew that she had family in Virginia, so a final stop in the Washington area seemed appropriate as well as productive.

Eileen interviewed Mrs. Gates; Mrs. Nathan Farragut Twining, wife of the Chairman of the Joint Chiefs of Staff; Mrs. Robert Anderson, wife of the Secretary of the Treasury; and Mrs. Morris Cafritz. Gwen Cafritz was a famous Washington hostess. Mrs. Cafritz explained to Eileen, as they sat sipping Spanish sherry in the Cafritz living room, why her dinner parties (always for twenty-two people) were so successful. She said that it was the guests who made a party, not the decor or food. Eileen dutifully reported that observation to her readers back home.

Eileen finished off her trip with a lengthy visit with Pat Nixon. On a sunny October day she went to see Mrs. Nixon in her handsome English Tudor home in Washington. After they had chatted for a while, Mrs. Nixon gave Eileen a tour of the house. During the tour Eileen talked briefly with the Nixons' older daughter, Tricia, and she peeked in on Tricia's younger sister, Julie, who was in bed with the flu.

Eileen wrote a long article describing the Nixon home and the many unique objects that the couple had collected on their trips abroad. The article came out in the *Union* on November 3. Accompanying it was a photo of Mrs. Nixon serving Eileen coffee from a silver coffee service. Eileen told Everett that she and Pat Nixon had a lovely visit over their coffee. She said they exchanged reminiscences about the Queen's recent tour, discussed their families, and, as always, had a great rapport.

When it was time to leave, Mrs. Nixon walked out to the street with Eileen. Duncan and I and our two little boys, ages four and six, had arrived to pick up our reporter/mother/ grandmother. I remember that Mrs. Nixon was wearing a bright-blue wool dress, and that she was warm and gracious when my mother introduced us all. It was a crisp but sunny autumn day (Eileen described it in her article as a "chill, autumn day," but then she was used to California weather), and the nearby trees were still covered with brilliant autumn leaves. As we stood there in the sun talking, a big black car drove up.

"Oh, here comes the Boss," Mrs. Nixon said. "Would you like to meet him?"

Vice President Nixon got out and came over to greet us. He was relaxed and genial. I'm sure he felt secure with us. Eileen had already established herself in his eyes as a sympathetic person, and Duncan and the boys and I must have looked like the quintessential American family. Duncan's and my two little sons shook Vice President Nixon's hand, and our four-year-old nearly shook him off the sidewalk.

"It must be fun to have little boys," the Vice President said.

That is a favorite memory of mine. Everyone was so at ease that day, and the day itself was so pretty. I know it was a happy moment in Eileen's life. She was proud of her recent achievement as a newspaperwoman, and she was pleased to have her family beside her as she chatted with the Nixons.

Eileen mailed Mrs. Nixon a copy of her article, and shortly afterwards she received a handwritten note in reply. In her letter Pat Nixon wrote:

> How sweet you were to write me a note in addition to the masterpiece for the paper. After reading both, I fear I have something to live up to! At any rate, I do want to thank you for being so generous.
>
> I enjoyed our visit ever so much and was filled with admiration that you were still in top form after your exhausting trip covering the royal visit.
>
> It was a real joy to meet your delightful family. I know how proud you must be of them and how

> difficult it is that the miles separate you. The next time you are here we'll have a family tea party.

*

Two years later Eileen spoke to Robert Letts Jones, vice president of the Copley Press, about her experiences on the Queen's tour. In a speech he gave in 1959 at the annual convention of the National Federation of Press Women, he quoted Eileen as saying:

> When I covered Queen Elizabeth II's tour two years ago, I noted that the most experienced reporters were not afraid to do what they had done as cub reporters. They tagged. They "dug." They worked. They pushed.
>
> Some of those schooled in the "movie" journalism often were content to follow the Queen by television in their hotel rooms, except on the big events. They held it was foolish to expend energy sitting on rooftops and walking blister-forming miles on any but important occasions.
>
> Yet, so often it was the so-called unimportant occasion, such as the tree-planting at Government House and the tour of the National Gallery in Washington, D.C., which revealed the Queen at her informal, human or cultural best.

Eileen flew home in 1957 knowing that she was one of those reporters who had dug, worked, and pushed. She had even sat on the roof of the Ottawa post office, to get a better view of the war-memorial service. At age fifty-one she had behaved in the best cub-reporter tradition.

Work and Play

Eileen came back to San Diego that October with a terrible cold. The events of the past few weeks had caught up with her. But she didn't intend to rest. Opening night of the opera was approaching, and there were dresses to describe.

On the way home from the airport she and Everett bought the October 28, 1957, issue of *Life*. In the upper right-hand corner of the cover was a small picture of Eileen sitting in the packed gallery of the Canadian Parliament, and down below was a large picture of Queen Elizabeth opening the Parliament. Everett said he now knew that Eileen really *had* been in Ottawa.

During the late 1950s Eileen covered many opening nights of the opera, and many symphony galas and benefit balls, but she and Everett also went to private parties, with their inner circle of friends. Among their favorite events were the "musicales" that Max Miller and Everett put on. Max had formed a group called the Miller Sisters' Band, in which he played drums and Everett played the trombone. Howard Chernoff, the former general manager of the *San Diego Journal*, was the violinist in the band.

This musical entity eventually evolved into a twelve-piece (yes, twelve!) instrumental group named the Mission Hills String Quartet, in which, strangely enough, Everett still played the trombone. One night three members of the group called Duncan and me in Virginia and performed a classical number for us over the phone. The trio consisted of Everett on the trombone, Howard on the violin, and an admiral named Admiral Pride on the bagpipes. Howard said he was hurt that Duncan and I couldn't seem to hear his violin!

The Mission Hills String Quartet and its auxiliary members

presented Everett with a trombone at a surprise party one evening. Everett had played the trombone in high school, but he hadn't owned one in years. He was content to rent one whenever the musical group met. Howard felt this situation couldn't continue. He formed a committee, which obtained donations. Then the committee purchased a second-hand trombone and had the names of those who had donated to the fund engraved on the instrument. The engraving was said to have cost more than the trombone itself. Everett wrote Duncan and me that now he no longer had an excuse for not practicing on his trombone "between engagements."

*

Eileen returned one more time to Washington, in the summer of 1958. This time she concentrated on her family, although she did have lunch with Betty Beale one day. Everett came east with her, and we all toured the sights of the Washington area. Everett liked seeing Virginia at last, the home of his ancestors. On our way to Monticello we stopped for gas at a station that was next to a historical marker. The marker indicated that the Confederates had won a battle there, that at that very spot they had wiped out a unit of Yankee soldiers from New York. Everett found that information very satisfying, but Duncan, who was a native of Albany, New York, was not so pleased.

That summer we visited Lowell Houser in his new Virginia home. Lowell had moved to the country estate of his brother, Theodore Houser, former president and chairman of the board of Sears, Roebuck. Lowell had worried that his bad heart might give out on him in San Diego and that he would become a burden to his friends. He retired from San Diego State and moved into Moss Neck Manor, his brother's Georgian mansion near Fredericksburg, Virginia.

Lowell, who was a wonderful artist, had lost his creative urge. Each day he prepared to draw or paint, and each day he did nothing. It hurt Everett to see his friend in such a state. Everett himself was as creative as he had ever been. He was still illustrating books for the Limited Editions Club and the

Heritage Press, and he was still painting nonstop. My parents felt that Lowell should have remained in San Diego, but they sensed that he would never come back to California to live, so they didn't try to persuade him.

Upon their return home, they made a major purchase: they bought a Dodge four-wheel-drive truck with camper. They had plans to explore more of Baja California and mainland Mexico, and they were now prepared to travel over the most rugged terrain.

On October 1, 1958, the Nixons came to San Diego for one day, to attend something called the "California Republican Roundup." Eileen and several other press women interviewed Mrs. Nixon in her suite at the El Cortez Hotel. In the interview Mrs. Nixon described her feelings during the frightening episode in Venezuela the previous May, when angry mobs spat on her and her husband and stoned their official cars.

Eileen wrote a long article after the El Cortez interview and as usual had many nice things to say about her Washington friend. Mrs. Nixon might get a bad press from some of the East Coast reporters, who apparently found her hard to know, but she could always count on Eileen to write about her with kindness and admiration.

On October 12, 1958, Jim Copley and his wife, Jeanie, gave a dinner party in their home honoring England's Lord Louis Mountbatten. Among the guests were Eileen and Everett and Ellis Spreckels Moore. Mrs. Moore and Lord Mountbatten were delighted to see each other again after thirty-eight years. They had first met in Ellis' Coronado home in 1920, when the Prince of Wales had dropped in with his cousin Louis Mountbatten for an impromptu visit. Eileen was happy to see her friend Ellis again, and to witness that meaningful reunion.

In December of 1958 Duncan and I moved with our family to San Diego. During Duncan's years with a public-relations firm in Washington, he had often asked Eileen's advice on how to promote certain products (Spanish sherry, for example, or coffee over tea). Eileen had sent him pages of ideas, and Duncan's boss, Sam Bledsoe, had followed almost all of her suggestions. Mr. Bledsoe began to depend on Eileen. He would ask Duncan to write her and get her thoughts on a certain subject. Back would come a thick envelope filled with her thoughts. Mr. Bledsoe couldn't believe his good fortune in having such a creative person as an unpaid consultant. To Eileen, coming up with promotional ideas was as easy as breathing.

Years later, in 1976, I was in Washington having dinner with the Bledsoes, and Mr. Bledsoe said to me, "And how is your mother? I never met her, but I felt I had. I remember her as being a most remarkable woman. Yes, a *most* remarkable woman!"

*

The pace of social life in San Diego got faster and faster as the decade of the fifties neared its end. Eileen was aware of the changes that had taken place since 1950. In some notes she wrote about the early fifties, she said that "second homes were on the increase," and that "the old-fashioned tea hour had bowed to the morning coffee because of heavy automobile traffic in the afternoon." The part about the vanishing tea hour was something she had pointed out to Duncan's boss in Washington in one of her many memos. In her notes she also said that "midweek parties were inching their way in, despite protests of husbands." By the late fifties Eileen was covering parties throughout the week. The husbands had definitely lost that battle.

As the sixties approached, social life in San Diego had become international. In 1958 Tijuana was first brought into San Diego's social picture when San Diego and Tijuana women met to form a Tijuana auxiliary to the Women's Committee of the San Diego Symphony. Eileen had much to do with the intermingling of the two social groups in the years that followed. To thank her for consistently promoting good Mexican-American relations, the *Comité Pro Sinfónica* of Tijuana awarded her a plaque in 1965, and in 1977 the Mexican and American Foundation presented her with its *Dama de Distinción* award.

*

In July of 1960 Eileen covered two national political conventions. The first was the Democratic convention in Los Angeles. Of the four political conventions she eventually covered, three were Republican and one was Democratic. Everett went along to L.A. and somehow made it through the hectic week. (He had broken out with eczema at the Republican convention in 1956.)

Eileen wrote reams of entertaining copy about the various "tanned and tousled-haired Kennedys," and the morning after John Kennedy was nominated for President she got a little scoop when she thought to telephone his mother. Actually Kennedy's press secretary, Pierre Salinger, had tipped Eileen off that "Mother Rose" was alone in her room at that moment and might like some attention. Eileen called her and interviewed her over the phone. Eileen said Mrs. Kennedy was very friendly. Perhaps the Irish name "Eileen" appealed to her and made her more willing to talk, or perhaps she liked the fact that Eileen was paying her some attention.

That same morning, right after John Kennedy announced that he had chosen Lyndon Johnson to be his running mate, Eileen and a few other reporters (Betty Beale among them, I am sure) tracked down Mrs. Johnson, in the Johnsons' hotel suite, and obtained an interview. Eileen wrote in her notes that "breakfast dishes had to be wheeled out to make room for us as we rushed in to get her reaction to the nomination."

Everett begged off on the Republican convention in Chicago. It was not that he didn't like Republicans. It was just that he didn't like large amounts of people, whoever they were and whatever they were doing. Eileen took her vivacious friend Jo Bobbie MacConnell along in Everett's place. Jo Bobbie said later that she had never seen Eileen "in action" before. She reported to her La Jolla friends that Eileen was an entirely different person when she was going after a story in a big-time setting. She was not the relaxed, warm-voiced lady on the phone at home, calling the people in her file for news. In Chicago, Jo Bobbie said, Eileen moved like lightning and was *very* determined.

Anyone who knows newspaper people well is familiar with that dogged, almost fanatical side to their personalities. The average person, who enjoys reading the newspaper each morning over coffee, tends to forget that the article he or she is enjoying so much is the result of some reporter's hard work. If the story involves a big event, like a political convention or a queen's tour—or a war—that story is the result of some real scrambling on the part of the reporter. Admittedly some members of the media have become unbearably aggressive in recent years. Still, when people knock the media, I always wonder if they realize how much of their entertainment in life, not to mention their information, comes to them because some reporter went after a story with ruthless determination.

In spite of traveling in the company of the terrifying "new" Eileen, Jo Bobbie had a grand time in Chicago. She and Betty Beale got along famously. After the convention was over, Betty visited San Diego. Eileen and Everett entertained her in their home and introduced her to many of their friends.

In September Eileen and Everett celebrated the end of the conventions by taking a trip to Mexico in their camper. They visited the pre-Tarascan ruins of Zacapu, in Michoacán, and also spent time in Guanajuato. On the way home they stopped in Mazatlán and went deep-sea fishing. Eileen, to her dismay, hooked and then was forced to land a ninety-pound sailfish. She wrote a series of articles for the paper about their trip, which Everett illustrated. That series earned Eileen a 1960 Copley Journalism award for "outstanding initiative and originality in reporting."

Bob and LaRue Thompson accompanied them on that long trip. The Thompsons drove in their own camper, but shared in all of the adventures. Bob was a member of the Mission Hills String Quartet and a genuinely gifted musician. Each evening on the trip he and Everett would sit beside the campfire and play their flutes (recorders) together.

Eileen and Everett often camped with the Thompsons after that, and with Ray and Irma Stoudt. Like Everett, Ray had been a charter member of the Miller Sisters' Band and then had gone on to play in the Quartet. But he was known for his virtuosity on the slide whistle rather than on the slide trombone.

In May of 1961 my parents introduced the Thompsons to

Laguna Hanson, in Baja California. Unfortunately, the lake, which had been so full in 1938 and 1939, was completely dry in 1961. Eileen and Everett were relieved to see that nothing else about the place had changed. The area, with its great white rocks and its pine trees, was still peaceful and uninhabited. The Thompsons appreciated the site, and they assured Eileen and Everett that they could visualize water in the lake.

*

During the early sixties Eileen kept turning out her daily columns and weekly editorials. Her "family" of file people was getting bigger all the time, and the parties she wrote up were getting bigger, too. By then she was using one of the rooms in her house as an office. She would phone the people in her file in the morning, start writing around eleven, and then take her copy to the paper in the afternoon. Eventually the paper arranged for a messenger to come by the house each day and pick up her copy. That made her job much easier. She liked having time to catch her breath before she had to start getting dressed to go out in the evening.

Eileen avoided luncheons whenever possible. Occasionally, when she was covering opening day at the races or some other major noontime event, she had to take a break from her usual schedule. But she preferred to phone and write during the day, and then go out at night.

Socially, the early sixties were just an extension of the fifties. Women still wore hats and gloves; a well-groomed, tidy look was in. (Witness Jacqueline Kennedy in the White House.) Eileen was still writing about a conventional society. Among a certain crowd in town, debutante balls were the big subject—whether to have them or not. San Diego, a notoriously laid-back community, couldn't seem to make up its mind. Women met and debated. Some of the groups backed off; some went ahead. Eileen noncommittally wrote up the balls that did take place, and described the young girls in their long white dresses. Within a few years many of the ex-debutantes were protesting the Vietnam War, dressed as hippies. Eileen's job then was to listen sympathetically to their mothers' agonized complaints. During those first years of the sixties, though, life went on pretty much as it had in the fifties.

*

Toward the end of the fifties Eileen and Everett inaugurated a tradition that would eventually become an annual social event for a number of San Diegans. They persuaded another couple to camp with them in Baja California over the Thanksgiving holidays. By 1960 the idea had caught on. Sixteen people, four of whom were children, drove about a hundred miles south of the border (a three-hour drive) and camped in a forest of live-oak trees, in a narrow valley that led to the sea. They ate their Thanksgiving dinner as the Pilgrims did: seated at tables in the open air.

In 1961 at least twenty-five people joined the camp. In 1963 there were so many campers gathered around the fire one night that the artist Ivan Messenger decided to paint a picture of the scene. His whimsical little painting, like Marius Rocle's at Laguna Hanson in 1939, captured on canvas the very essence of a camping trip in Mexico.

As the years passed, more and more San Diegans chose to celebrate Thanksgiving in Baja California. Occasionally the group did meet in the United States. Twice the campers spent the Thanksgiving holidays in a California desert, and one year they congregated on the Ramona property of Eileen and Everett's good friends the Philip Gildreds. All the rest of the camps, however, from the late fifties to the mid-eighties, took place below the border.

In 1966 Eileen wrote in her column:

> Statistics were staggering in regard to one of the largest November holiday encampments ever held under spreading oaks 30 miles south of Ensenada. This traditional Thanksgiving getaway, which does not represent a club or organization, has been growing. This year the party numbered 74,

> including 32 children (without a quarrel) and seven dogs (without a snarl).

In 1968 the camp was starting to look elegant. Eileen wrote:

> This year ... [it] had everything but a French crystal chandelier. The long line of linked tables set up under venerable ... oaks, was graced with monogrammed linen napkins, silver candlesticks, bird of paradise blooms and other urban appointments.

Each Thanksgiving people arrived in a variety of rigs. Some were large and fancy; others were small and Spartan. The most intriguing was the one owned by two of Eileen and Everett's favorite Baja companions, Bob and Dolly Maw. Bob had designed and built their futuristic camper, which opened up like a clam shell.

In 1972 eighty-nine people appeared in camp. The oldest person was in her late seventies; the youngest was a two-year-old. The oldest was Margaret Bancroft, widow of Griffing Bancroft, the gentleman who had sent his squab sailing through the air at Ellis Spreckels' famous dinner party. Margaret was a rugged camper. By day she caught and bridled local horses for the children to ride; at night she slept in a tent, which she had pitched herself.

The event continued to attract large crowds for the next six years, but by 1978 rain had become a problem. As the first campers approached the oak grove in November of 1978, they discovered that the normally dry riverbed in the valley had turned into a rushing stream. The running water didn't bother them—they managed to ford the stream in several places on their way to the oak grove—but the heavy rain that was falling was another matter. The rain kept falling all that day and all that night. It fell the next day, too, and the next night. Many people feared that when the time came to leave they would be unable to ford the rising stream and make it back to the highway. They all made it out safely, however. The following winter huge rainstorms hit the area. The stream turned into a raging river that almost filled the valley. The water uprooted three-fourths of the ancient oaks and sent them crashing down the valley to the sea.

The year after that storm the Thanksgiving camp attracted fewer people, even though the rains had subsided. The toughest campers came back, though, and they continued to come back for a number of years.

In its heyday the encampment resembled a large gathering of gypsies. It was a harmonious gathering. People cooperated with each other; everyone tried to be of help. Some men sawed big logs for the campfire. Others shot quail in the surrounding hills for their friends' consumption. Two veteran campers, Orrin Klapp and Payne Johnson, offered music—guitar and banjo playing—as their contribution to the group. On several occasions Mr. Music himself, Bob Thompson, brought along a full-sized Mexican marimba, which he set up under the trees and played each afternoon.

The food was always delectable. Besides quail, the campers dined on fresh lobster, bought from local fishermen. Emma Lee Powell, one of Eileen and Everett's dearest friends, provided her fellow "gypsies" with homemade biscuits baked in her camper oven. Several women served the group luscious homemade tamales. Each year on the Saturday night after Thanksgiving, Clayton Brace, owner and general manager of San Diego's Channel 10 TV, cooked crêpes suzette for everyone.

The camp brought different age groups together at a time when generational mistrust was the rule in the United States. Long-haired college students mingled with retired military men. One day several Stanford youths sawed some logs, aided by a cheerful, sturdy older man. Later, as the young men walked away, one of them commented about their helper, "You know, General English sawed more logs than any of us. He's a really good guy—even if he is a Marine general!"

Camp stories became legends. People still talk about the "Great Owl Hunt." No actual owl was involved; it was merely a chance for everyone to wander through the woods together at night and hoot. Then there was the time a boat came into camp.

A San Diego husband and wife were ready to leave town on Thanksgiving morning when they discovered that their rented camper had serious mechanical problems. Determined to eat turkey with the rest of us, they moved all their food and gear to their cabin cruiser, which was moored at the San Diego Yacht Club. They then transferred their cruiser to a trailer and towed it south.

Several people who arrived in camp the next day were startled to see a large boat cozily nestled among the trees. One man, who had missed its arrival Thanksgiving Day, swore he was going to give up drinking when he unexpectedly came upon it in the woods that night.

Whenever the campers would meet during the rest of the year, at various San Diego social functions, they would immediately gravitate to one another. They had become more than "social acquaintances." They had bonded under the oak trees of Baja.

The Thanksgiving camps ended in 1985, when Eileen and Everett's camper finally gave out. *They* didn't give out at that time, but their truck did, and they felt they were too old to buy another.

Today Eileen and Everett's grandchildren and their friends (all those nonquarreling children that Eileen wrote up) still camp in Baja and in the California mountains and deserts. They learned about camping from two unique individuals, and now the younger members of those long-ago camps are carrying on the tradition.

The Pack Rat and Questions of Etiquette

In the spring of 1960 a jewel thief began operating in the San Diego area. He was a clever thief. He seemed to know exactly which houses would contain jewels and which would be unoccupied at night when he arrived to rob them.

The thief always spaced his robberies, perhaps in order to catch his victims off guard. He would steal some jewels and then wait several weeks, or even months, before he struck again. Just as the local citizens would start to feel secure, believing that he had left town, another robbery would occur.

After a while the police began to suspect that he was burglarizing the homes of people whose names appeared in Eileen's column. Every time a house was robbed, the police would discover that Eileen had mentioned in the paper that the owners would be attending a social event that night. The police felt the burglar was depending on Eileen's column to tell him who the rich people in town were, and when they would be going to a party.

The burglar was nicknamed the "Pack Rat Burglar," for he often deposited packages in a post-office storage box. Those packages would contain items that he had stolen but felt he should not keep, items of sentimental value to the owners—lockets with baby pictures in them, wedding rings, and so on. In other words, the Pack Rat was a burglar with a heart. He was still a burglar, however, and the police were eager to catch him.

Besides sending back some of the valuables he had stolen, he also showed consideration in another way: he never threw objects about or disturbed the general order of a room. One of the victims of his crimes admitted that he seemed to have taken care not to break her Dresden figurines when he ransacked her jewelry case. He appeared to have moved her china pieces carefully to one side. LaRue Thompson, however, was less impressed. She said the burglar had kicked her pearls under her bed when he had robbed the Thompsons' house. Pearls were apparently not on his list of easily fenced gems. LaRue was glad he had left the pearls, but didn't see why he had treated them so disrespectfully.

Once word got out that the police thought the thief was using Eileen's column to pick his victims, many of her friends in San Diego and La Jolla hesitated to tell her about their social plans. Suddenly Eileen was finding it hard to get news. At that point she and the police decided to combine forces to catch the thief.

As part of the trap, Eileen printed a list of names of people who were going to attend a certain event on a specific night. Then, the night of the party, the police staked out the homes of the people on her list. The burglar got lucky. That evening he did not rob a house. He continued to frustrate the police for several more weeks. On the occasions when they were waiting for him, he either robbed an empty house or he did not rob at all. But at last, on an October night in 1961, the trap worked. That night the police caught the burglar in one of the houses whose owners Eileen had mentioned in her column.

After the burglar's conviction and sentencing, in January of 1962, Eileen asked the police if she could meet and interview him in jail before he went off to prison. She said she had some questions to ask him. The police agreed and arranged a visit.

Eileen wrote an article about the Pack Rat episode in her life. She had intended to submit it to a magazine, but she decided to incorporate some of it into one of her columns instead. In that article she said:

> Our column stands convicted with the man who read it daily for 18 months to successfully burglarize an estimated 108 houses in our area—homes in most cases of our personal friends. The police estimated his haul amounted to $50,000. We take comfort in the fact that our column, which

served him, also helped to catch him.

There have been other compensating factors, not the least of which was the professional advice on "how not to get robbed," which he gave us to pass on to his victims … He said this information was his way of paying his debt to Society—fashionable Society, that is, which he had burglarized, held in nightly terror, fascinated, mystified and often charmed, for a year and a half. He indicated he felt less obligation to society in the wider community sense.

In the advice he gave us to pass on to what he called his "offended persons" he suggested that women stop stuffing their jewels in their lingerie, in corners of their dresser drawers, in shoe boxes and in stored suitcases. He thought the trash can, the middle of the table under the morning newspaper, the rafters of the garage were among the safest caches. Garages, particularly messy ones are overlooked usually by jewel thieves, he said.

"The householder who is going partying and who doesn't want to take all his cash with him ought to fold it within the daily newspaper and lay it carelessly on the kitchen table," he advised, adding with the flash of humor he occasionally showed, "but he should remember, when he comes home, half crocked, not to throw the whole thing in the garbage or fireplace."

He believes locked doors and windows are deterrents to burglars … and he admitted in our long interview with him that most thieves will avoid a house guarded by a dog.

He told us he liked pretty things and hated to see them destroyed wantonly, and his pattern confirmed this.

"When I had time I always looked around to enjoy the pictures and statues but I tried not to take or harm anything I couldn't sell," he said.

"Then you didn't deliberately kick Mrs. Thompson's pearls under the bed as she said you did?" we asked.

"Yes, I kicked them under the bed," he confessed. "I didn't want her to step on them when she came home and entered a dark room. She wouldn't expect them to be there.

I didn't have time to put them back in her case, so I kicked them out of the way. They were worthless to me but I figured they might be important to her."

The list of those invited to identify their stolen goods reads like a social roster. Since it did, we decided to cover the assemblage at police headquarters as a major social event. We announced the 10 a.m. session as a "morning coffee," that party being currently popular in social circles here. The police met the lighthearted challenge with wit and did serve coffee (in paper cups).

Pack Rat, now safely in jail, had been shown the advance story on the "morning coffee" by the detective sergeant in charge. Pack Rat said he ought to have been invited to come as the party's social lion.

Victims obviously were disappointed not to meet him face to face that morning. They arrived modishly dressed, women wearing well-tailored suits necessarily accented by rhinestones (they hoped to find, and some did, the real thing in the loot to be identified).

Two girls found their engagement rings. Squeals of happiness occasionally pierced the "party" as victims recovered heirlooms or other items that Pack Rat had not found time to return, via the post-office storage box. One delighted guest was a wealthy socialite who located her 28 books of green stamps with as much glee as if she had found the pendant for which she also was looking. She said 12 of the books were missing, but Pack Rat insisted to us he had never "turned in" any books at stamp headquarters. It developed he had taken them for the same reason his victim had saved them—to use toward Christmas presents.

Pack Rat is sentimental about Christmas. He told us he had never stolen during the holidays and had never snitched a Christmas present.

He easily could move in the social circles he reads about and in a less clandestine way than that which landed him where he is. He … could pass for a stockbroker, a doctor or an associate professor of literature (which he likes) or a sportsman (which he is).

Pack Rat has innate, rather than showy manners. He was quick to rise to put our wrap around us when our interview in the County jail offices was at an end.

When we protested that the steam-heated room was warm and we did not need the coat, he smiled [and said]: "Permit me, it may be some time before I have an opportunity to put a wrap around a lady's shoulder again."

For our professional comfort he assured us that he would miss reading our column.

In a letter Eileen received from the Pack Rat after her interview with him he said:

I hope your friends will not think too badly of me, and that some of the information I gave you will compensate somewhat for my wrongdoings. It was nice talking to you and breaking up a somewhat monotonous routine.

Eileen answered his letter, saying:

> Thank you for your note and courteous interview. At this time I am not writing anything for publication but am passing along your advice to some of those involved.
>
> I got in touch with a Catholic Monsignor who said he would have a priest contact you. I hope this faith gives you the support you need.

Eileen rather liked the Pack Rat, but she was happy that his career had ended. He was sentenced to prison for a term of ten years to life. She felt better knowing that a man of his professional skill would no longer be reading her column for professional reasons.

*

In November of 1960, while the Pack Rat was still on the loose, a woman arrived in town whom Eileen had often quoted but never met. On November 2 Eileen dedicated most of her column to the etiquette authority Amy Vanderbilt. Miss Vanderbilt had given a lecture in San Diego the day before, which Eileen had attended. In her column she referred to Amy Vanderbilt as "America's new queen of etiquette."

Eileen enjoyed Miss Vanderbilt's talk, and she particularly liked her definition of "what a lady is today." Eileen wrote approvingly in her article:

> Miss Vanderbilt says: "[A lady] is … one who thinks primarily of others' feelings, who looks and acts in the manner of the best of her group. She does not brag about her possessions or financial worth."
>
> Miss Vanderbilt's credo emphasizes "a lady is neither a social climber nor a social snob. She is never afraid to enlarge her social circle to include others whose social background may have been different but whose social and moral worth are unquestioned by other intelligent people.

> "A lady does not apologize for her friends nor speak ill of those whose hospitality she has accepted ..."

People often called Eileen to ask her advice on questions of etiquette. If she was unsure how to answer, she would consult an etiquette book, and in 1960 the book she consulted the most was Amy Vanderbilt's. Eileen felt that Miss Vanderbilt's approach to manners was not stuffy and staid, but up-to-date and practical. Eileen agreed with Amy Vanderbilt's statement that "manners are ... a practical way of making living happier for us all."

Eileen herself took RSVPs very seriously. In her editorials she often advised her readers to RSVP promptly when invited to a party or a wedding. My mother was a relaxed social arbiter on many matters, but where RSVPs were concerned she could be quite stern.

*

In 1962 Eileen wrote another series of travel articles for the *Union*. That summer the U.S. State Department sent Everett on a trip. He was to serve as a visiting professor and to make an evaluation of the College of Fine Arts at the University of Costa Rica.

Eileen went to Costa Rica with him, and on the way they again visited Mayan ruins in Guatemala and Honduras. Lowell Houser was able to join them, so the trip reunited the three good friends. Eileen wrote several articles about the ruins, which Everett illustrated. They were becoming a travel-article team. Eileen would describe the places they visited and the adventures they had, while Everett would make sketches of the scenery, the people, and the ancient buildings.

When they arrived in San José, Costa Rica, the tables were turned on Eileen. *She* was the new celebrity in town. One of the leading professional women in Costa Rica gave a tea for her. At the tea the press interviewed her, asking her many questions about her experiences as a reporter. The paper *La Prensa Libre* referred to Eileen as "*la distinguida periodista norteamericana, dama encantadora.*" In a letter Everett wrote to Duncan and me, he reported that she was a sensation in Costa Rica. He said that everyone loved her.

Eileen loved the Costa Ricans, too, but she preferred to write rather than be interviewed. Soon she had escaped from the enthusiastic newswomen of San José, and had begun writing articles again. This time she described the social life and customs of the Costa Ricans and the volcanoes in their country. Her stories on Costa Rica were syndicated and appeared in newspapers around the United States. After three weeks Eileen reluctantly returned to San Diego, leaving Everett to finish his work at the university.

*

In 1963 a major change took place in Everett's life: he retired that June. He didn't have to retire so soon, but he wanted to devote more time to painting. In some ways he was sad to leave his job. He enjoyed teaching, and he loved his students. He always said that his years as a professor at San Diego State were some of the happiest of his life.

That summer Eileen and Everett went on another camping trip, but before they left Eileen wrote one of her most endearing editorials. She received many letters from her readers complimenting her on it. It appealed to everyone who had ever rooted for a child in Little League. In her editorial "Little League Social Etiquette" Eileen said:

> Little League activities properly belong, we suppose, on the sports pages or in files of the sociologists who have had plenty to say about them. Social scribes are remiss to neglect them since they, in one season, represent more two and three generation gatherings (on spectator benches) than a dozen festive Yuletides, more hot dog picnics than a month of Fourth of Julys, and more neighbor togetherness than all the morning coffees on the block in a year.

We've been introduced to this social phenomenon this season by two grandsons who play … and if we have a missed a game they know it.

We've learned a lot about baseball and more about social etiquette on the bench.

First rule is one fundamental to all spectator sports—don't say mean things about a player, you may be sitting next to his father, or worse, his grandmother.

Our first observation was that the pitcher on the opposing team looked like a Padre player taking advantage of all the little fellows. The man sitting next to us assured us he was only 12. He said he ought to know—he was his Dad.

Good sportsmanship among baseball spectators isn't a virtue. You not only can be partial, you're obligated to root only for your own team.

When we applauded a good catch by a member of the opposition, a bench companion, devoted to "our side" observed: "Lady, this ain't tennis."

It's considered ladylike and quite all right to yell (all the best people do it) but you're supposed to know the lingo.

Correct observation for a home-run is "That ball is g-o-n-e." When you want to stop a steamroller team you yell to your side "put out the fire."

"That's watching, son" is a nice thing to scream when the player refuses to strike at just anything, or "that's the old eye out there—make him find it." When you want your team to start a rally you resort to this one: "Let's make it a merry-go-round."

"What a wipe-out" is proper talk when the score is 14 to 2, which it often is. You never lose heart … Anything can happen and usually does.

Our friend Dan Burnham's experience is one we can appreciate. When he arrived late his Little

> Leaguer son told him, through the field fence, that the score was 24 to 0.
>
> "Don't worry, dad, we haven't been up yet," the boy assured his father.
>
> Fashions vary but slacks seem to be favored by the young hatless mothers. Men tend to be more fashionable at the mid-week games because they come direct from their offices in well-tailored business suits. If you dress up too much everybody notices it and you feel just as miserable as if you had gone in "black tie" formality to a picnic.
>
> When we stop by the field en route to a cocktail party we always add a disguise—old shoes and old coat, extras which we keep in the car. This way we achieve correct casual chic.
>
> There are after-the-game-is-over manners too. You don't rush up to kiss your winning grandson even if he is only nine and even if you are his grandmother. And you learn not to say too much if there are tears in the eyes on the way home from the lot.
>
> It's all right, though, to take your emotions out on the "ump." Everybody does.

After Eileen wrote that editorial, she and Everett, accompanied by the Thompsons, joined Everett's brother and his wife on a camping trip in Utah, Arizona, and Nevada. They returned home glad to have explored those places, but convinced more than ever that they preferred Mexico. In her editorial "On Finding 'The Better Place'" Eileen wrote:

> Mexico is more challenging. They don't fence you … there and you camp on your own, sometimes with luck or worry, often with beauty, always with freedom of choice. There the "better place" is elusive, leading you on and on.

In October of 1963 Eileen and Everett were back in Mexico, camping in Baja California with a small group of friends. As they were about to break camp on a Sunday morning, someone erroneously told the rest of the campers that daylight-saving time had ended that day. Daylight-saving time would actually end the following Sunday, but no one challenged the speaker. In her editorial entitled "Eternity In An Extra Hour" Eileen described what happened next. She wrote:

> Over a campfire in the pines of Baja California early last Sunday morning someone in camp announced that daylight savings time ended that day.
>
> "How fortunate, I can think of no place in the world where I'd like better to spend an extra unexpected hour," said one of his companions. This companion believed the erroneous report which no other camper in the group cared to dispute.
>
> It proved to be a great hour, "an agreeable addition" which all unexpected hours should be, according to the poet. It was not wasted in that "Vain Pursuit of This and That Endeavor and Dispute," but it was wonderfully wasted by some, and wisely spent by others.
>
> On the basis of the new knowledge that he had an extra hour the painter in the party went back to the bold boulders which he had been painting, and he painted like sixty for another sixty minutes. His wife finished the who-dun-it which her conscience would not permit her to read when she returned to her work-a-day world.
>
> The camper who always packs with order gave even more attention to dismantling camp gear. He reassembled it with leisure and confessed that he broke camp this day without his usual sense of depression.
>
> The careful camper almost singlehandedly

erased signs of the camp and left smoldering logs which he knew for sure would never spark a pine needle.

Then there was the young, sensitive camper who took time to go back for a last lingering look at the watercress-choked stream winding through delicate willows and wild roses.

Perhaps, he and the painter were most enriched by the poet's advice: "to see a world in a grain of sand and heaven in a wild flower—hold infinity in the palm of your hand and eternity in an hour."

The extra hour proved that it could be practical as well as poetically agreeable. Unworried the campers made greater haste than usual and arrived at the Tecate border before closing even if unaware that they never had had an hour to lose.

We wonder if they will do as well with the extra hour dividend which actually comes to them today.

*

After that restful camping trip, Eileen came home and started preparing for an out-of-town assignment. The publisher of her paper, Jim Copley, was sending her to Miami Beach, Florida, in November to cover the social aspects of the 1963 Inter-American Press Association (IAPA) convention. Its delegates would represent the major newspapers of North, Central, and South America. As usual Eileen's job would be to concentrate on the women at the convention. She was to pay particular attention to the wives of the leading publishers of Latin America.

Eileen knew that she was also going to cover the IAPA convention in 1964, in Mexico City. Jim Copley wanted her to attend both conventions so she could check out the hospitality offered in the two cities. He was planning ahead, for in 1965 the annual IAPA convention would be held in San Diego.

In November, while Everett flew to Texas to visit his relatives, Eileen flew to Miami. A veteran now at covering conventions, she felt that this was going to be one of her easier assignments.

Four More Conventions and Europe at Last

As Eileen had suspected, the IAPA convention of 1963 was easy to cover. However, neither she nor the delegates and their spouses could have predicted its sorrowful ending.

The convention began the night of Monday, November 18, in the ballroom of the Americana Hotel in Miami Beach. It began with great excitement because of the presence of its featured speaker, the President of the United States.

Eileen filed articles throughout the week. She interviewed a number of Latin women, most of whom were the wives of publishers. A few, however, were magazine and newspaper editors, women with careers. She also wrote about the parties—the luncheons, picnics, and yachting cruises—that the host city had organized for the wives' entertainment. Eileen's most memorable article, though, was the one that came out on November 25, after she had returned home. In it she described the contrast between the festive opening night of the convention and the somber closing dinner. In this article, entitled "'Triste' Mood Marks Closing of Conference," she wrote:

> Social life of the Inter-American Press Association Assembly closed where it began—in the ballroom of the Americana Hotel, Miami Beach—but with a dramatic difference that every guest … will remember as long as he lives. The gala spirit of the first banquet a week ago tonight and the tragic "triste" mood of the last gathering Friday were occasioned by the same man—the 35th President of the United States, John Fitzgerald Kennedy.

> Many of the guests [who were] headed for the ballroom last Monday, where the late President was to speak, were held up in the crowded nearby lobby by elaborate security precautions of the Secret Service. Because of security restrictions all of us—delegates, guests and observers—had been listed and cleared. The lobby jam permitted many of us to get an informal close-up view of the President before we heard him a few minutes later address the IAPA. The boyish, vigorous President, his hair characteristically tousled, tried to give every roped-off lobby guest a personal greeting. A few minutes later he had made a quick change from his business suit to a dinner jacket and had, as all the women noticed, combed his unruly hair.
>
> He entered the ballroom (a room as festively dressed as the women guests) to a standing ovation. In the same setting Friday night, a few hours after the assassination of this young President, these same convention guests, representing the major newspapers and magazines in the Western Hemisphere, arrived sobered and stunned in somber black They dined quietly, after a standing invocation, at flowerless tables. Toasts, farewell speeches and entertainment had been cancelled. Unsmiling guests left the tables to pack, carrying home with them the handsome souvenir program of last Monday's dinner.
>
> A headline the next morning in the Miami Herald said simply: "Only five days ago …"

Eileen told her family that almost every Latin woman at the final dinner was wearing a black dress and a black lace mantilla on her head. Eileen said she was amazed at the ability of the Latin women to adopt an instant mourning mode. She also told her family that she was glad she had been running late the night of the opening dinner. Otherwise she would have missed the

President's personal greeting in the hotel lobby.

*

In 1964 Eileen covered two conventions: the Republican national convention in San Francisco in July, and the IAPA convention in Mexico City in October. Everett remained in San Diego that July, so again Eileen went to a convention by herself. She wrote in her notes, though, that in San Francisco there were so many San Diegans present she felt as though she were "covering a Christmas crunch circuit at home." She was delighted to see Betty Beale again, and as usual the two had fun as they covered the various social events together.

The Goldwaters often visited San Diego and La Jolla, so Eileen's articles featuring Mrs. Goldwater were simple to write. She was writing about a woman she already knew and liked. The same could be said, of course, about Pat Nixon. At a large fashion-show luncheon that was given that week, Eileen sneaked in a few words with Mrs. Nixon. In writing about the luncheon and the two women, Eileen said:

> Mrs. Barry Goldwater, wife of Sen. Goldwater, who opposes Gov. William Scranton for the Republican presidential nomination, was greeted yesterday by a standing ovation at the … fashion show luncheon of 1,750 women given at the Fairmount Hotel by the California convention Host committee.
>
> … Mrs. Goldwater was obviously delighted by the applause which almost turned a lady-lovely, non-partisan luncheon into a rally. She was becomingly modest and composed, as always.
>
> Mrs. Nixon was a queen herself at this coronation. She admitted to us she enjoyed the release from the strain of being in a tense spotlighted position during a campaign. She looked rested, and fresh as a daisy.

Eileen managed to ask a few "political" questions of some of the women she talked to at the convention. For example, she asked Mrs. George Romney, "Is there a division of ideas too great for your husband to join Sen. Barry Goldwater in an all-out effort for the presidency, if he is nominated?"

Mrs. Romney hastened to assure Eileen that Governor Romney would "never bolt the party." Eileen had never been known to ask questions like that before. She had clearly picked up a few tricks from Betty Beale.

In October Everett traveled with Eileen to Mexico City. He knew he would have no trouble finding things to do while she covered her second IAPA convention. That October Eileen renewed her acquaintance with many of the women she had met the year before in Florida, and she interviewed several new women, including a woman editor from Argentina and one from Peru. She also wrote an article about the four women who were simultaneous translators at the convention. The *Union* ran all of her stories about the IAPA convention, and Mexico City's English-language paper, *The Mexico City News*, ran them, too. When the convention was over, Eileen obtained an interview with Emma Hurtado Rivera, the fourth and last wife of the painter Diego Rivera. Everett was more than happy to accompany Eileen on that assignment.

Señora Rivera had married the famous artist in 1955. He was fighting cancer at the time and died in 1957. Eileen reported in her article that Emma and Rivera had been friends for ten years before their marriage, and that during those years she had "served as his art agent in the little gallery below the painter's last home."

As Eileen sat in that home, talking with the painter's "effervescent, Titian-haired" widow, she couldn't help thinking about the young bride who had almost met Diego Rivera thirty-eight years before. In 1926, when Eileen was only twenty years old, she and Everett had decided not to join Mexico City's sophisticated "studio crowd." But now she was a poised, capable woman in her fifties, a woman who had worked on a newspaper for more than three decades. She was used to dealing with sophisticated people. Eileen wished Diego Rivera were still alive.

She would have enjoyed meeting him in 1964, and she might even have asked him for an interview.

Before my parents returned home that October, they went to see the pyramid of Cholula, and they visited the cities of Puebla, Papantla and Jalapa. Eileen wrote some articles for her paper about those places, and Everett illustrated them.

*

In the spring of 1965 Eileen and Everett finally got to Spain. They had hoped to go to Spain much earlier, but Eileen's unexpected pregnancy plus the Depression and World War II had affected their travel plans.

After the war ended, Eileen kept mentioning Europe to Everett, and he kept ignoring her hints. He preferred to journey south. He was not only enamored of Mexico and the countries of Central America, but he also had a practical reason for wanting to visit that part of the world. In the 1930s he had begun teaching a class in Pre-Columbian art, and by the time of his retirement he was known as an authority on that subject.

In 1965, however, he was a retired professor, without the excuse of his work to influence Eileen. She insisted that it was time they both learned something about the countries their friends were always visiting. After Everett reluctantly agreed to go to Europe, they made plans to visit Portugal, Spain, France, and England. They would spend a few days in Portugal and several weeks in Spain. Then they would end their trip with three days in Paris and three days in London.

Eileen was happy and excited as she prepared for this new adventure. Nothing could bother her, not even the comment of one of her well-traveled friends, who said, "Oh, you're going to Paris for the first time? What a pity that you'll be seeing it for the first time *now*. It's practically ruined now, you know! It was so much better before the war!"

Eileen wisely remembered that all places were better "before." Just recently she and Everett had shaken their heads sadly when a young couple had returned from Chapala and had raved over its beauty. Eileen and Everett knew that Chapala had been much more beautiful in the 1920s. They felt sorry for that young couple, who could only know it "now."

Eileen had heard from her worldly friends that since all the new airplane luggage looked the same lately—slate-gray plastic suitcases were popular in those days—travelers should make a distinguishing mark on each piece before they left home. That way they could easily identify and claim their luggage in the airports.

"Everett, dear," Eileen said, "please make a distinguishing mark on each of our suitcases. Paint a slash of color or something."

Everett obliged with artistic fervor. Around each gray suitcase he painted a gorgeous white, yellow, and bright-blue snake. Its feathered body wound around the suitcase, and its tail appeared next to the handle. It was, Everett explained to Eileen, Quetzalcoatl, the plumed serpent of Mexico. "He will guard us on our trip," Everett said, which was how Eileen and he went to Europe, but took a little bit of Mexico with them.

Naturally they fell in love with Europe. They found Portugal enchanting, and then they lost their hearts to Spain. They drove all over Spain in a rented car, from the Altamira caves in the north to Andalusia in the south. Eileen wrote some inspired articles about the Feria of Seville and about Cuenca, the clifftop city of "hanging houses" in new Castile. Everett must have felt inspired, too, for he created some of his most beautiful drawings to illustrate her articles.

At a certain point on the trip, in one of the caves of Altamira, Eileen was holding a flashlight so that Everett could sketch some of the cave paintings. Eileen noticed that a man was standing near them, and that he was staring at her. "Say!" he exclaimed, as he caught her eye. "Aren't you Eileen Dwyer? I went to San Diego High School with you!"

The man no longer lived in San Diego, and he hadn't seen Eileen for over forty years. The fact that he had recognized her, and in a cave in Spain, of all places, proved how little she had changed since her girlhood.

Eileen and Everett couldn't get over the kindness and courtesy of the Spanish people. They first became aware of

Spanish helpfulness when Everett left his wallet and passport at a desk in the Madrid airport. He discovered his loss when he and Eileen were on a bus going into the city. Suddenly they were aware that a car was following the bus, and that the driver of the car was honking furiously. When the bus stopped, a young Spaniard leaped from the car and ran up to the bus door. "Here is your wallet, *señor*! And your passport!" he cried.

The gracious behavior of the Spaniards continued to the very last, when Eileen and Everett drove back into Madrid after their trip around the country. Everett had no idea where he was and where their hotel might be. He asked two young men in the car next to them how he could get to the hotel, and they said, "Follow us!" They then led my parents for miles through Madrid until they reached the hotel. The Spaniards drove off with a merry wave of their hands. "No trouble!" they called. "No trouble at all!"

Eileen and Everett also lost their hearts to Paris. "The French will cheat you," someone had told them. After their first cab ride in Paris, Everett overpaid the driver. The French currency had confused him.

"No, *monsieur*!" the cab driver insisted, and he began thrusting bills back into Everett's hands.

A San Diego friend who lived in Paris devoted himself to Eileen and Everett while they were there. He gave them a personally guided tour, and showed them places they would never have seen on their own.

Then, in London, another wonderful thing happened. Eileen informed Everett that they would be taking a bus tour the first day, since they did not have a friend in London to show them the city. Everett disliked the idea of a bus tour. He was sure he would hate the experience. But when they entered the bus that morning, they discovered that except for themselves and their guide, every single person on the bus was a Mexican. Soon the other occupants of the bus had accepted Eileen and Everett as fellow Mexicans, and before long, in between the guide's lectures, Everett was singing *ranchera* songs with his new *compadres*. Eileen said later that only Everett could find a busload of Mexican tourists in the middle of London.

"But then," she added, "he probably had some help from Quetzalcoatl."

She reported to her family that the Portuguese, the Spaniards, and the French had reacted calmly to the Quetzalcoatl suitcases. But, she said, the English baggage handlers had dissolved with laughter when they saw those snakes.

*

Eileen and Everett came home from Europe and almost immediately found themselves hobnobbing with royalty. On June 3, 1965, they met and had lunch with the Prince of Tonga. Their host was Howard Chernoff, former general manager of the *Journal* and violinist extraordinaire in the Mission Hills String Quartet. Howard had recently been working in American Samoa as a TV consultant, and while there he had met the Prince of Tonga. The Prince, who was planning to bring TV to his island kingdom, needed advice on how to build a television station.

Howard was happy to advise him. In return he asked if the Prince could provide the San Diego Zoo with some three-foot-long Tongan iguanas. Howard had recently served as president of the San Diego Zoological Society, and he knew that the zoo could use some of those exotic lizards. The Prince obliged, and then, on a shopping trip to the United States in 1965 (Eileen wrote in her notes that he shopped for seaplanes in Oregon and a coconut-shell-cracking machine in New Jersey), he came to San Diego to see how his iguanas were doing.

Eileen wrote that the Prince weighed three hundred and seventy-five pounds, was six feet four inches tall, and wore a size twenty collar. She said that he was very interested in viewing contemporary American kitchens. She reported that he asked for an armless chair at the restaurant where the luncheon was held, as he couldn't fit into the chairs with arms. When the waiters brought him his chair, he called it a "throne."

*

On October 8, 1965, the twenty-first annual convention of IAPA began in San Diego. This convention, which would last a week, was the one Eileen had been preparing for. Jim Copley and his new bride, Helen, were co-chairs of the convention's host committee. Eileen had given them her suggestions, based on what she had observed in Miami and in Mexico City.

After studying the hospitality efforts of those two cities, she had recommended that San Diego offer social events that would include all the out-of-town guests, not just the IAPA board members and their spouses. The Copleys accepted her recommendation, and as a result found themselves committed to giving a dinner for five hundred and twenty-five people rather than for sixty. The dinner took place in the tented garden of their beautiful La Jolla home on October 13. Eileen wrote in her notes that their party was not only the "social climax" of the convention, but also one of the loveliest parties ever given in the San Diego area.

Throughout the week of the convention, Eileen filled her columns with descriptions of the other entertainments that the host committee had provided—the luncheons (one held on the aircraft carrier the USS Kitty Hawk), breakfasts, and sherry hours. By then Eileen knew most of the out-of-town visitors. She had met them in Miami Beach, seen them again in Mexico City, and now was greeting them for the third time. She wrote long columns about the visitors and their activities. She wrote vividly and prolifically, and her writing reflected the happy atmosphere of the convention itself. Anyone reading her columns that week would think that she hadn't a worry in the world, that her only interest in life was the IAPA convention and whether it was going well.

Writing those sprightly columns was a remarkable feat on her part, for on September 29, approximately one week before the convention started, my husband, Duncan, was in a serious automobile accident. He died a day later, on September 30. Somehow Eileen managed to provide her family with care and emotional support, while simultaneously preparing for, and then writing about, a major international event.

A Kind and Hard-Working Galley Slave

Everett once wrote some notes about Eileen in which he said, "If there are two most obvious characteristics connected with her writing they would be dedication to hard work and kindness to people."

Eileen continued to live up to that description as she wrote her columns and editorials in the late 1960s. She did work hard, and she turned out prodigious amounts of copy. Her column, which was a long one, appeared every day, and it contained news about people in all parts of the county. She wrote up engagements, weddings, trips, and parties—and she was always kind.

In Robert Letts Jones's 1959 talk to the National Federation of Press Women, he had quoted Eileen as saying that she felt the good reporter should have faith in people and not a cynical attitude toward them. She had added, "This may make her or him seem naive, but I sincerely believe this faith is reflected favorably in the copy."

One of Eileen's acquaintances, a society writer on a paper in San Francisco, once teased her about her "kind column."

"Eileen," the woman said, "I could never write the sweet stuff you write. No one would read it. It would never go over up here!"

Eileen laughed, because she genuinely liked that San Francisco newswoman, but she had no intentions of changing her style. Eileen cared about her readers too much to want to gossip about them. She considered that her job was to record the happy moments in their lives and to promote their benefit functions. Over the years many women told her that their benefits would not have "made it," that they would not have been successful, without the publicity she gave them in her column.

Today, when so many women work and receive pay for their labor, it is hard to remember that years ago a whole group of women worked but never brought home a paycheck. They were the volunteers of the community. They were more than mere "points of light." They were an army, and one wonders who is doing all that volunteer work now. The causes were worthy, and in most cases the volunteers were worthy, too. If a few women got into the act for less than noble reasons—a desire to improve their social status, for example—who really cared? The cause was served, whatever the motive of the volunteer.

Eileen always assumed that *everyone* had a pure motive. If a society matron asked her to help "sell" a certain fund-raising event for sick children, or for the arts, and so on, Eileen was quick to push the event in her column. She would list the people who had already promised to attend (after 1960 she made a point of getting their permission first; the Pack Rat had taught her to do that), and she would describe how glamorous and wonderful the event was going to be. She would plug it and plug it until the party-going public would know that whoever missed *that* event would miss The Party of the Year. Amazingly enough, Eileen was able to pull this off time and again. She liked helping those women, for they were her friends and she wanted to see them succeed. Also, she approved of their causes. Eileen had a strong sense of civic pride, perhaps because she was a native San Diegan. She admired those volunteers, who worked so hard. She felt that any woman who helped the charitable and cultural institutions of San Diego flourish deserved publicity.

*

On April 15, 1967, Eileen was sixty-one years old, but she still had the instincts of a cub reporter. That April she found a way to meet and interview the mystery writer/attorney Erle Stanley Gardner, creator of the Perry Mason mysteries. "Uncle Erle," as he liked to be called, had a home, Rancho del Paisano, in Temecula, sixty miles north of San Diego. Eileen knew one of his best friends—an old-time San Diegan, Roscoe (Pappy)

Hazard. Pappy told the writer about Eileen. Mr. Gardner was a Baja California enthusiast, and when he heard that Eileen was, too, he invited her up to his ranch.

She had a good long visit with him and wrote two in-depth articles about him. Her stories, which were syndicated and printed in numerous papers, were very popular with her readers. She received many letters congratulating her on her stories about "Uncle Erle," and she also received several letters from the mystery writer himself. She told some of her friends that she had enjoyed interviewing a man for a change. She always got along with the women she met, and she always wrote intelligent, entertaining articles about them. But she liked proving to her editor that she could also write intelligently and entertainingly when her subject was a man.

*

In 1965 Eileen had persuaded her reluctant husband to go to Europe. Two years later she thought it would be nice to go there again, but she agreed with Everett that first they should introduce their grandsons to the country where they had honeymooned.

In the summer of 1967 Eileen and Everett took their older grandson—a teenager, not quite sixteen—on a month-long, five-thousand-mile automobile tour of Mexico. They wanted to show him some of their favorite places in what was still their favorite foreign country. Eileen wrote a series of articles about the trip, entitled "The Byroads of Mexico," which Everett illustrated.

The following summer, in 1968, they headed south again and spent a month in Chapala with their younger grandson. They rented a large, picturesque house in the center of town. The house belonged to the painter Peter Hurd, and had once belonged to the poet Witter Bynner. They had admired it in 1926, but had never dreamed that they would ever live in it. Their friends the Thompsons and the Phillips, and also Eileen's brother, Bill Dwyer, came down to visit them while they were in Chapala. Eileen said the Witter Bynner House, as people still referred to it, was such a rollicking, happy place that summer, she almost felt she was back in her honeymoon villa, El Manglar.

After they returned home, they found that everyone was talking politics. America was in the middle of a tumultuous Presidential campaign. Eileen, as usual, was only mildly interested in the political situation, but she was very hopeful that the election results would favor her Washington friend. That fall she had the satisfaction of knowing that Pat Nixon would soon be the First Lady of the United States. Eileen did not cover either of the conventions in 1968, but in November, after the election, she wrote a glowing article about Mrs. Nixon that was syndicated and printed in papers throughout the country.

*

In 1969 Eileen and Everett went back to Europe. That summer they took the Quetzalcoatl suitcases to Germany, Greece, and Italy. The letters and postcards Eileen sent home were lyrical. No one ever appreciated foreign sights and foreign experiences more than she. She wrote several travel articles about the trip, which the *Union* published.

In Venice Eileen interviewed the aging but still vital and attractive heiress and art collector Peggy Guggenheim. Eileen and Everett spent an enjoyable afternoon with her in her palazzo on the Grand Canal, viewing her large collection of twentieth-century painting and sculpture. Everett reported that they both fell in love with her. Eileen had read her biography, and she was fascinated to meet the real person. In Eileen's article about Peggy Guggenheim she wrote:

> Familiar with details of her sophisticated Bohemian life described in minute detail in her astonishing biography "Out of This Century," published in 1946, we were disarmed by her quiet refined charm and her tentative shy approach, belied now and then by a roguish smile.

Everett made a sketch of Ms. Guggenheim's palazzo, which the *Union* printed next to Eileen's story.

*

Over the years many San Diego groups honored Eileen for her accomplishments. She was named a "Woman of Valor" in 1959 and a "Woman of Elegance" in 1968. Then in 1969 she received what was perhaps her most cherished award. The San Diego Chapter of Theta Sigma Phi, a national professional society for journalism and communication (later called Women in Communication), presented Eileen with its "Galley Slave Award," in recognition of "the galleys of type it would take to tell of her service to the people of San Diego." The Theta Sigma Phi write-up about the award summarized Eileen's life and career, saying:

> … her influence has reached far beyond the soon-to-be-forgotten lines of type on newsprint. For years she has made it a special objective to foster genuine friendship and cordial social relations among leaders of Tijuana and San Diego
>
> … She has untiringly supported San Diego's cultural growth and often has brought success through her column when it appeared an event might fail.
>
> Describing her community influence, her husband Everett Gee Jackson (who as an artist and professor of art at San Diego State has never been called "Mr. Eileen Jackson") notes, "She has come very near to making most of the people of San Diego into one great, happy, loving family, who can't stand not to see each other almost every day." Accompanying Eileen to the parties she covers—sometimes one each night of the week—he knows whereof he speaks.
>
> … In addition to her column, Eileen has written many travel features on Mexico, Central America

> and Europe illustrated by her husband.
>
> She also has written a weekly "Social Editorial," ... which gently raps gauche manners or applauds graceful acts and civic contributions.
>
> ... Eileen regards "Straws" as more than a social column. "I like to think that many years from now the column will reflect the way we lived at this time ... that it will be a little social history."

*

The year 1970 began with a bang: Eileen and Everett became grandparents again. They had already acquired a third grandchild in 1967, when I married Tom Williamson, a widower with a nine-year-old daughter named Tabi. Then, in January of 1970, Tom and I had a baby girl. Eileen was delighted to have a fourth grandchild, although she feared that she and Everett would not live long enough to know her very well.

"I'm almost sixty-four," she said, "and Everett will be seventy this year. We're too old. We'll be gone before Hildy grows up."

Happily, both Eileen and Everett lived to see their granddaughter Hildy grow up, graduate from college, and begin her adult life. From the time she was born, it was obvious that she was one of their greatest joys.

*

That same January Eileen met Abigail Van Buren, when "Dear Abby" came through town. Eileen had always admired her for writing an advice column that was both witty and wise. Having once been a "Dear Abby" type herself, as a teenager on the *Sun*, Eileen had a special feeling for advice columnists. But of all the ones she had ever read, Abby was by far her favorite. She was glad to learn that Abby in person was just as witty, vivacious, and charming as her column had made her out to be. Abby, who was featured on the cover of the January 1970 issue of *Family Circle*, gave Eileen a signed copy of that magazine. Across her picture on the cover she wrote, "To Eileen the

Beautiful—Abby Van Buren."

Abigail Van Buren was one of several well-known figures who appreciated the loveliness of Eileen's face. Bertrand Russell had told Eileen she was gorgeous as he chased her around a kitchen in 1931. Upon meeting Eileen at a ball in Coronado one year, the movie and swim star Esther Williams had exclaimed, "Mrs. Jackson, you're beautiful! You know that, of course." The TV journalist Barbara Walters had had a similar reaction to Eileen when the two met in the home of Jeanne and Clayton Brace. Ms. Walters had commented to her hostess on Eileen's "great beauty." A famous songwriter, too, had apparently noted Eileen's face, at a party in La Jolla. As proof that my mother was not always up on her celebrities, she didn't know who the man was, even after she learned his name.

"There was this little skinny man there playing the piano," she informed her family, "and he kept telling me how beautiful I was. He said he wanted to write a song to me."

"But who was it?" we asked.

"Oh, I don't know. But he must have been important; everyone was fawning over him. His name was Hoagy something or other. Somebody said he'd written a song called 'Star Dust.'"

Eileen always seemed surprised when people told her she was beautiful. She was one of the least vain women I have ever known. She was so busy accomplishing things, she didn't have time to dwell on her looks. She did believe in being well groomed, and she did color her hair and wear lipstick to the end of her life. But she never worried about the wrinkles that gradually appeared on her face. With her cheekbones, she didn't need to.

*

In the spring of 1970 Eileen and Everett's friend Howard Chernoff persuaded them that they should go across the Pacific Ocean for a change. Howard had a new job. He was now the U.S. ambassador to the Japan World Exposition—Expo 70—in Osaka, Japan. Because of Howard, Eileen and Everett decided to join a group of San Diegans on a Chamber of Commerce Mission to the Orient. Clayton Brace would head the mission, which would leave in April. The group would stop first in Japan, to take in the fair, and then would visit Hong Kong. It was to be a working vacation for Eileen, as the paper wanted her to write more than just travel articles. She was to cover the trip from start to finish.

She had begun writing articles about Expo 70 in September of 1969. Back then, when she was starting to inform her readers about the exposition, and when Howard Chernoff was busy preparing for it, Howard had passed along some interesting information to Everett. He had told Everett that the Japanese were going to sell various edible products at the exposition, and that they planned to name some of their edibles after famous citizens of the United States. Howard said that he had put Everett's name on the list of prominent Americans, and that the Japanese had promised to name a candy bar after him. It would be called the "Everett Jackson" candy bar. In spite of the fact that Everett would have a painting and a lithograph on exhibit in the American Pavilion, Howard had not stressed that Everett was an artist. "Everett Jackson is the world's greatest trombone player," Howard had told the Japanese officials.

When the San Diegans arrived in Osaka, Howard greeted them with much fanfare. He informed them that he had declared that day, April 14, "San Diego Day" at the exposition. Throughout their stay he continued to treat them all like VIPs. But he ruefully explained that something had been lost in translation regarding Everett's candy bars. He presented Everett with a box of them. The candy was rich and delicious, but the name of the candy bar, written in bold Roman letters on each wrapper, was not "Everett Jackson." It was "Trombone."

*

Besides writing her columns and taking trips, Eileen covered two important dinners in the early seventies. The first took place in September of 1970. It was a state dinner for more than six hundred guests at the Coronado Hotel. It had the distinction of being the second state dinner ever given outside the White House.

President Nixon was honoring President Gustavo Díaz Ordaz of Mexico, and included at the dinner were former President and Mrs. Lyndon Johnson, cabinet officers from both countries, Governor and Mrs. Ronald Reagan, and the Nixons' daughter Julie, and her husband, David Eisenhower. In some notes she wrote about the party years later, Eileen said:

> Also present were several ill-fated guests, part of the Watergate scandal and tragedy which forced President Nixon to resign. These guests included Attorney General John Mitchell, his wife, Martha, H. R. (Bob) Haldeman, and John Ehrlichman.
>
> I telephoned Martha Mitchell before the dinner, in San Clemente, and found Mrs. Mitchell "irrepressible and completely natural" when I asked her what she would wear to the dinner. She explained: "You know what? I never know what I'm going to wear until I have to put it on. What are they wearing down there?"
>
> I noted in the press that Martha "probably will go down in history as the nation's most outspoken, protocol-shattering cabinet officer's wife in history."
>
> During our telephone conversation she invited me to come up and shake her hand at the dinner. I did.

The second major party that Eileen covered at that time was held in January of 1971. Jim and Helen Copley gave a dinner in their home in honor of Prince Juan Carlos of Spain and his wife Princess Sophia. Today, of course, they are the King and Queen of Spain. Eileen and Everett were included among the fifty guests.

President and Mrs. Nixon had honored the royal couple at a White House dinner two days before. Eileen called Betty Beale in Washington and found out what the women had worn at the White House party and who was there. She then incorporated that information into her own stories about the Prince and

Princess. Eileen and Betty were a good team, even when separated by three thousand miles. In talking with the Princess, Eileen was able to tell her that she had interviewed her mother, Queen Frederika of Greece, in 1953.

*

The *Union* continued to give Eileen exciting assignments in 1971, but in one way the year was a sad one for both my parents. Lowell Houser, their merry-hearted companion for so many years, died that winter, at Moss Neck Manor in Virginia. It was reported that he died in his sleep "with a smile on his face." Eileen and Everett admitted that that was a good way to die, but they still were devastated that Lowell had left them. A few years earlier Max Miller had died, so by 1971 Eileen and Everett had lost two of their closest friends.

In April of 1971 they took a trip to a place that they felt Lowell would have liked. They traveled to the Mexican town of Creel, in Chihuahua. From there they went down into the *barrancas*, or canyons, of which the Copper Canyon is the most famous. In June the *Union* printed what many people considered to be one of the best articles Eileen had ever written.

Her article was partly about the trip, but most of all it was about the Tarahumaras, the semi-nomadic "gentle cave people of Mexico." Eileen thoroughly researched her subject, so the article was not only filled with descriptions of the Tarahumaras, but also with information about them. The response from her readers was immediate and positive. She received many letters thanking her for writing such an article. The readers thanked Everett, too, for the sketches he made to go along with Eileen's story. San Diego seemed to have fallen under the spell of the Tarahumaras, those swift-footed, quiet, mysterious people.

*

In August of 1971 Eileen was invited, along with several other reporters, to tour the Western White House, in San Clemente, California. Pat Nixon was waiting for them. She welcomed all of them to her home, but saved her warmest greeting for Eileen. The two immediately began chatting together, in their usual compatible way. As Mrs. Nixon led the group on a tour of the house, she confided to Eileen that she was longing for grandchildren.

During that same West Coast visit, the First Lady transferred some acres of federally owned land next to the Mexican border to the state of California for a beach park. She arrived at the site in a dramatic fashion, by helicopter. Later, after the ceremony was over, she endeared herself to a group of Mexican children on "the other side" by impulsively ordering a portion of the fence to be cut so she could reach over and embrace the children. She also had her picture taken next to a bearded, long-haired surfer. In the picture a group of people surrounds her as she stands next to the surfer and his surfboard. It's a happy scene. Everyone in the photo—including Eileen, in the background—is either grinning or laughing.

Eileen's article about the event at the border inspired a note of praise from one of the executives at her paper and an irritated letter to the editor from a disgruntled San Diego woman. The woman wrote:

> Eileen Jackson, in her article on Pat Nixon's visit here, must have devoted a good two-thirds of the story to Mrs. Nixon's choice of clothes.
>
> If you must print that antiquated irrelevant drivel, at least you could confine it to that useless wasteland, the women's section.

The times were changing, and Eileen's kind of column was facing an uncertain future. However, she wasn't bothered by the criticism. She knew there were still women around who wanted to read about a First Lady's wardrobe. Eileen also knew that she wouldn't be writing forever. A new generation of reporters would take over someday, and they could write however they pleased. Meanwhile she would continue to describe women's outfits. After all, in her article on the Tarahumaras she had written:

> The women in this cave wore colorful cotton … dresses with peasant blouses. Sometimes when they come to Creel they wear their entire skirt wardrobe, one skirt on top of the other, sometimes as many as seven.

Whether her subject was a Tarahumara woman or the First Lady of the United States, Eileen was prepared to describe her clothes.

*

In the fall of 1971 Eileen and Everett spent two weeks in Ireland, traveling over a thousand miles by car. Eileen's articles about Ireland, like so many of her travel features, were syndicated. Her article about Lake Gougane Barra, and about the little island in the lake that is associated with the life of Saint Finn Barr, was particularly popular. It appeared in a number of papers. Eileen wrote that "hordes of tourists go to the lakes of Killarney, 50 miles away, but poets, writers and artists seek Gougane Barra."

Everett may have been one of those artists who sought Gougane Barra, but he did not make any drawings while he was in Ireland. He said that driving in that country took too much out of him, that at the end of each driving session he had no energy left for sketching.

When Eileen and Everett had gone to pick up their car at the Irish rental agency, the agent had informed them that Everett was too old to drive in Ireland. Eileen would be able to drive, the agent said, but not Everett.

Eileen could be unreasonable at times. Everett always insisted it was an Irish trait. Few people knew about her unreasonable side, for she was the soul of reason at work. But there were certain things, she told her family, that she *could not*—and therefore, *would not*—do. For example, she could not balance her checkbook, nor could she turn on a radio by herself. No one could persuade her that she was capable of doing both those things. She had a tendency to throw checkbooks up in the air when Everett tried to teach her how to balance her account, and even though she had no trouble turning on a TV set, she persisted in her belief that switching on a radio was too complicated an act for her to understand.

"I will *not* drive that car!" she whispered to Everett as they walked to the back lot where the Irish rental car was waiting. "They drive on the left in this country, and *I can't do that*!

"Well, at least you'll have to drive the car away from *here*," Everett told her, "or they won't let us have it. I'll drive from then on, and hope I don't get caught."

"I will not drive that car *anywhere*!" Eileen said.

Everett sighed. "OK. Give me your hat, then, and you lean down in the car and stay out of sight."

They climbed into the automobile, and Everett put on Eileen's lavender wool hat with the frilly veil. Then, scrunching low in the seat, he slowly drove the car past the plate-glass window of the agency's front office and on out into the street. After he had gone a few blocks, he sat up straight and gave Eileen back her hat.

Everett said it was bad enough to be driving for two weeks on the "wrong" side of the road in Ireland, but it was even more disconcerting to be driving illegally. Eileen was unconcerned. The illegality didn't bother her one bit.

"And that," Everett told her, "is because your ancestors were named 'Lawless.' It's easy to see how they got that name!"

Countdown To Retirement

In 1971 Eileen decided that she would work for five more years. Everett had retired from the college at age sixty-two, but that was because he wanted to concentrate on his painting. Eileen thought that she should stop writing her column and her social editorials when she was seventy.

She was determined to make the most of the next five years. She was going to work hard, and she was going to have fun with Everett. She planned to travel with him as often as possible. With one notable exception, the days of my parents' big trips—to Europe, to the Orient—were over. But they didn't feel deprived. They returned to Mexico and found new places to explore. As always, Mexico satisfied them completely.

In the spring of 1972 they took another long trip with Bob and LaRue Thompson. The two couples drove down to Guaymas, on the mainland of Mexico, and then put their campers on a ferryboat and crossed over to Santa Rosalía, in Baja California. From there they drove to the tip of Baja. After they had explored that region, they took a ferry back to Guaymas from the Baja city of La Paz, and drove home to California on the paved roads of mainland Mexico.

In February of 1973 Eileen and Everett traveled by air to Yucatán, and in a rented car visited Uxmal, Mérida, and Chichén Itzá. Then they continued on to Palenque, in Chiapas. In October of that same year they drove in their camper three hundred miles south of the border into Baja California to see the famous boojum (or Cirio) trees. Their good friend Norman Roberts, who would soon co-author a book on the plants of Baja California, had encouraged them to go and view those strange, surrealistic trees.

In the spring of 1974 Eileen and Everett traveled four hundred miles into Baja and camped for a month beside the Gulf of California at Bahía de Los Angeles, which Eileen called that "fish-filled royal blue bay." Four friends joined them on that trip: Bob Kellner, who had gone to Texas A&M with Everett; Bob's charming, adventurous wife, Gen; John Dirks, a sculptor, whom Everett always referred to as "old Proteus, god of the sea;" and John's wife, Ruth, a gentle, laughter-prone poet.

A year later, in 1975, Eileen and Everett and the Kellners drove five hundred miles south and spent a month in the Baja California town of San Ignacio, a place Eileen described as "an oasis of Arabian date palms in the midst of a lava rock desert dominated by the most photographed Spanish mission church on the 800-mile-long Baja peninsula."

Eileen wrote articles for the *Union* about each of those five trips—usually a series of two articles per trip—and Everett illustrated them. Now that he was back where people drove on the correct side of the road, and where he could drive legally, his energy level had risen and he was able to sketch again. Eileen's story about the Great Pyramid at Uxmal, in Yucatán, was syndicated and appeared in various papers around the country.

*

In between her trips Eileen continued to write up San Diego parties and weddings. Such events never ceased to enchant her. She felt that each party she attended was fabulous, and that each wedding she covered was almost unbearably beautiful. This attitude, which both amused and mystified Everett, kept her from going stale. Her copy always sparkled, because she never tired of her subject matter.

Eileen thought each wedding was beautiful, but she had to admit that in the 1970s they were not all alike. In those days many young couples were choosing to recite their vows in unusual places, wearing unusual outfits. Eileen went along with the trend. Some of her readers might not have known it, but she was really quite flexible where the new mores were concerned.

She had reason to be. After all, the first wedding she ever covered was held in a tiny plane three thousand feet above the city.

Occasionally a wedding came along that presented her with a special challenge, not because it was unconventional, but because it was so newsworthy. In the summer of 1972 she scooped the world with her copyrighted story about the marriage of the Princess of Thailand and a young San Diego man who was a close friend of one of Eileen's grandsons.

The bride and groom had met while they were students at MIT. Apparently the King and Queen of Thailand disapproved of their eldest daughter's decision to renounce her royal status, marry an American, and live the rest of her life in California. They did not attend the wedding, which took place in an Episcopal church in San Diego.

The bride's uncle was present, however. He told Eileen that the family wanted no publicity, that if the wedding had to be written up, Eileen was not to mention the names of the bride's parents. Eileen explained to him that she *always* mentioned the names of the bride's parents when she wrote up a wedding. She pointed out to him that the news was going to get out somehow, and that other reporters might not be as careful as she would be. She reminded him that the week before, *Newsweek* had printed a false rumor that the Princess was involved in a romance with a "wealthy Puerto Rican."

"Now wouldn't it be nicer," Eileen said, "for me to write up the wedding accurately and tastefully? It will be an important day for the bridal couple, and their wedding story should reflect that fact."

The bride's uncle sighed and said, "Mrs. Jackson, you are a charming woman, and you are *very* persistent!"

He gave Eileen permission to mention the bride's parents in the article, but he insisted on reading the article before it was printed, to make sure it was as accurate and tasteful as Eileen had said it would be.

Eileen was pleased to have scooped every other publication in the world on that story, and she was even more pleased, as the years went by, to see that the couple's marriage was a happy one. The bride's parents mellowed as grandchildren appeared. The

King and Queen maintained close contact with the California branch of their family, and they encouraged the Californians to make frequent visits to Thailand. Eileen was glad that things seemed to have worked out so well; she liked stories to have happy endings.

*

In October of 1973 Jim Copley died. He and Helen had had a happy marriage, too, but theirs had lasted only eight years. Eileen was deeply saddened. She had considered Jim her friend as well as her employer. Helen, with admirable grace and fortitude, took over as publisher of the *Union* and the *Tribune*, and as chief executive officer of the Copley Press.

In December of 1973 Eileen covered another local wedding of more than local interest. On that occasion a young La Jolla woman, Cheryle Ann Gaillard, married Major General Walter Robert Tkach, who was the personal physician of President Nixon. President and Mrs. Nixon and their daughter Tricia came to La Jolla to attend the wedding. As might be expected, Eileen gave that event special treatment. Her story plus the wedding photos took up almost half a page in the society section of the *Union*. In her article Eileen sadly reported that unfriendly demonstrators were clustered outside the chapel as the guests walked in, and that the "chanting of the demonstrators could be clearly heard during the ceremony."

By then the Watergate scandal had the country enthralled. People could talk of nothing else. Eileen took an interest in the proceedings—she would have been abnormal if she hadn't—but she was worried about Pat Nixon. The previous summer she had written Mrs. Nixon a letter of encouragement, and had received an appreciative letter in reply. Eileen was holding good thoughts for her friend. She hoped that, somehow, they would help.

*

In March of 1974 a royal visitor came to San Diego. On March 14 Prince Charles of Great Britain sailed into San Diego harbor on the British frigate the HMS Jupiter. He was serving in the Royal Navy at the time, as a communications officer, and he was taking part in a round-the-world training mission.

Several days before he arrived, Eileen wrote a long article about the other Prince of Wales who had visited San Diego, Prince Charles' great-uncle, the late Duke of Windsor. Eileen again recounted the story of that prince's two-day visit in 1920. She wrote that while he was in the area he attended a banquet and ball at the Coronado Hotel and popped in on Ellis Spreckels in her home. Eileen reported that Wallis Spencer was living in Coronado at the time, but that no one seemed to know whether or not she was present at the ball.

On the evening of March 14 Eileen and Everett went aboard the HMS Jupiter. The skipper of the ship, Commander J. P. Gunning, and its seventeen officers gave a reception that night for a hundred and twenty guests. In her column Eileen wrote:

> The guests aboard the Royal Navy frigate were mostly military officers, members of the British communities of San Diego and Los Angeles … and a few civic leaders from both areas and their wives.
>
> … Guests were warmly greeted by Cmdr. Gunning and the officers, including the one all eyes sought—Prince Charles. He was completely accessible and as easy to meet as he was to spot. No formal receiving line had been set up. Guests tended to form an informal circle around the prince, who was on host duty, as were the other officers.
>
> We had a long informal chat with him at the beginning of the reception and found him an engaging, composed and really handsome young man with a vast curiosity. He was interested in Coronado and talked about Hotel del Coronado (he didn't know quite where it was) where, he understood, his great uncle, the former Prince of Wales, was entertained in 1920. Prince Charles hadn't done his homework on that visit and seemed

> fascinated by hearing details of it, including the fact that the present Duchess of Windsor lived here at that time.
>
> Prince Charles seemed to us as casual and friendly as his father, Prince Philip, whom, on Oct. 12, 1957, we lightheartedly invited to come to California and bring Queen Elizabeth II … Last night, Prince Charles discussed seriously the route his parents might follow if they were to visit here coming from Western Canada.
>
> … Prince Charles has the keen blue eyes of his parents and a "fine head of hair," dark brown, modishly cut …

The next evening the Prince attended two receptions. The first was given aboard two linked Canadian destroyer escorts that were docked at a San Diego pier. At that reception the Prince received on the HMCS Gatineau. Later he moved on to the second reception, at a local officers' club, which was hosted by the British Officers' Mess of San Diego.

At the reception on the Gatineau an incident occurred which impressed me when I heard about it. My mother was making her way toward the Prince when a little man, who had an official look, stepped up to her and reminded her that she had already talked to the Prince the night before. He said that at this reception the Prince was to mix with people who had not had a chance to meet him before. When Eileen explained that she was a member of the press, and that she just wanted one quick word with Prince Charles, the man let her move ahead. Everett, who had missed hearing this conversation, tried to follow Eileen, but the little man indicated that Everett was *not* to move ahead. The man practically elbowed Everett aside, in his effort to keep Everett away from the Prince.

Everett was a proud man and a gentleman. He was not used to being elbowed aside, not even when a prince was involved. Everett turned away and walked over to the railing of the ship. He stood there looking out at the harbor, as he tried to compose himself. Suddenly he was aware that Prince Charles was standing next to him.

The Prince had met Everett with Eileen the night before, and now he said, "I read your wife's article this morning, and I enjoyed it very much. I bet you helped her write it!"

Prince Charles had noticed Everett's encounter with the little man, and had also noticed Everett's reaction to the treatment he'd received. After talking to Eileen for a minute, the Prince had left his spot at the party and had come over to soothe Everett's feelings.

"You mustn't mind that man," he said to Everett. "He's with Scotland Yard, and he's always following me around." When the Prince and Everett parted, both were smiling.

I have always felt that that was truly a princely gesture on Prince Charles' part. Many people have criticized him for neglecting his lovely wife, but I will always consider him a sensitive, thoughtful human being, because of his kindness to my father.

*

Eileen worked hard for two more years. She still had a devoted following, and she gave her readers what they seemed to like. When she wrote up a party, she would describe the setting in sensuous detail, as well as the dresses that the women guests were wearing. As always her genuine enthusiasm for the party and for its hosts would enable her to write fresh, enthusiastic copy.

She would describe flowers:

> The spectacular soiree Saturday was bursting with exotic floral beauty flown in from Hawaii … more than 500 shining red anthuriums, some massed in a high floral fountain … The visual experience included torch ginger, shell ginger, green and red ti leaves, monasteria leaves from the breadfruit plant … and 60 hanging baskets of begonias.

She would write about food and make the reader's mouth water. Recalling the delicacies offered at one party, she said:

> Tender crepes were filled with crab and avocado, chicken with walnuts, mushroom and spinach, Italian meats in Ruffolo and with Mornay sauce.

Describing the food at a more rustic affair, she wrote:

> Raw vegetables from the ranch garden tumbled decoratively from bushel baskets. The chef carved 500 pounds of beef, which had been cooked on hickory and oak coals in brick pits for 14 hours. The country fare included buttermilk biscuits, corn on the cob floating in milk, zucchini, pinto beans and cucumbers in sour cream.

She would continue to write about "black chiffon dresses, vibrant rose jersey dresses, stylish mauve sheaths, dresses of a rust and gold brocade."

Eileen's columns from those days were reminiscent of her letters home from Mexico in 1926, or of her postcards sent from Europe: they were all lushly descriptive. I feel sometimes that she was wasted in the twentieth century. Eileen, who could describe Thanksgiving camp and make it sound like a picnic at Versailles, would have had such fun in, say, the court of Louis the Fifteenth of France. Imagine how she would have written up *his* parties, how she would have described a dress worn by Madame Pompadour.

In 1975 Eileen covered a party that featured an eminent guest. Mrs. Gerald Ford, the nation's new First Lady, arrived in town on May 20 to cut the ribbon opening the Asian Galleries at San Diego's art museum. The first sentence in Eileen's article about Mrs. Ford's visit catches the reader's attention. Like so many of her first sentences, it makes the reader want to read on. She began her article:

> Great art is enduring and it can afford the

> partial eclipse it got last night at the Fine Arts Gallery when First Lady Betty Ford, distinguished special guest, took the spotlight at the Fine Arts Society's glittering 50th anniversary celebration.

After describing dozens of dresses, including that of the First Lady, Eileen reported that guests "found Mrs. Ford graciously accessible as she mingled with them at the pre-dinner cocktail reception."

In October of 1975 two more distinguished visitors came to San Diego. On October 10 Emperor Hirohito and Empress Nagako of Japan toured the San Diego Zoo and the Scripps Institution of Oceanography. Eileen was part of a thirteen-member reporting team that wrote about their visit.

The following year Mrs. Ford returned to California, and on May 6, 1976, she attended a cocktail reception in La Jolla. The party, which was held in the garden of a private home, was a fund-raising event for President Ford's Presidential campaign. Male staff writers on the *Union* covered the party as a news story, but Eileen concentrated on the beauty of the garden and, of course, on the beauty of the women's dresses.

That same month and year, May 1976, Eileen met and wrote about her eighth and last First Lady, or First-Lady-to-be, in this case. In the spring of 1976 former California Governor Ronald Reagan was campaigning for the Republican Presidential nomination against Gerald Ford. On May 13 Mrs. Reagan came to San Diego. It was her turn to attend a local garden reception. This one was a daytime event, a large garden luncheon. Nearly four hundred guests assembled to meet Mrs. Reagan and to ask questions of her. Eileen got to her first, however, with some questions of her own.

Eileen had a friend named Dorothy Tyson who was active in the Reagan campaign. Dorothy was a special friend—she was the fourth bride to be married in the Jackson studio—and because she was such a good friend she arranged for Eileen to ride to the garden reception in the same car as Mrs. Reagan. Eileen sat in the backseat with the future First Lady and asked some fairly probing questions. Eileen said that Mrs. Reagan seemed nervous during the interview. She had no reason to be, for Eileen ended up writing her usual kind column. In an article that came out on May 14, she said:

> Fine-boned Nancy Reagan ... behaves like a gentlewoman, is "refined," well-born and well-reared. She fields even provocative questions quietly and gracefully.

On May 28 Eileen covered a fund-raising cocktail party for Ronald Reagan, in La Jolla. Mrs. Reagan was unable to attend that party, but Eileen reported in her column that Ronald Reagan arrived looking "ruddy, slightly tanned and ... younger than his 65 years ..."

Eileen had celebrated her seventieth birthday that April. Her final column was scheduled for July 4, so she knew her days of writing about people like the Reagans and Betty Ford were almost over. She was therefore pleased that such an impressive trio had come to town that May.

*

As Eileen's day of retirement approached, an article about her appeared in the *Union*. It was headed: "'Straws in the Wind' Will Retire with Author." The *Union*'s publisher, Helen Copley, gave a brunch for ninety people in her garden in honor of Eileen. Included among the guests were former colleagues from Eileen's days on the *Sun* and on the *Journal*. Some were people she had known for more than fifty years.

Her readers sent her letters as Retirement Day loomed. They told her how much they would miss her column, her social editorials, and her warm voice on the phone asking them for news. They were sure no one could ever take her place. Eileen assured them that her replacement would do a wonderful job. She meant what she said. She was crazy about the man who was going to replace her.

It could have been a sticky situation. The Grand Lady of the Press retires and is supplanted by a man in his forties, who is known for his brilliance and wit. Eileen could have resented Burl Stiff, but she adored him instead, and she greatly admired his writing skills.

Burl took over the column, now no longer called "Straws in the Wind," and he made some changes. "Mrs. John Smith" became "Mary Smith" when he described her; he rarely wrote up weddings; and he expanded the scope of his column to include social groups that Eileen had missed. Eileen thought everything he did was perfect. On the occasions when Burl asked her for advice, she was happy to help him. They couldn't have had a more congenial relationship. The two remained good friends to the end of Eileen's life.

When Eileen retired, in July of 1976, she and Everett promptly went to Mexico. They had already made arrangements to rent a house in Chapala with Bob and Gen Kellner, the couple who had camped with them at Bahía de Los Angeles in 1974 and at San Ignacio in 1975. Eileen and Everett would spend their wedding anniversary in the little town where they had honeymooned fifty years before.

Retirement—for a While

Eileen and Everett and the Kellners spent two months in Chapala in the summer of 1976. This time my parents had chosen to rent a modern house. It faced the lake, and, unlike the complicated, romantic Witter Bynner House, it was all on one floor. In Chapala Everett painted while Eileen took long walks with Gen, planned and cooked the meals with her, and read mystery novels.

Shortly after their arrival in Chapala, the foursome read in *The Mexico City News* that Pat Nixon had had a stroke. Eileen immediately wrote her a note, joining the thousands of other well-wishers who sent Mrs. Nixon messages during her illness.

Away from the nightly sumptuous dinners of San Diego, Eileen lost weight. She was thrilled. She felt she had put on too many pounds in the years leading up to her retirement. Now she could report with pride that she was her old slim self again.

Just before Eileen and Everett came home, they visited the little town of Ajijic, where Everett had lived in the twenties. In a fancy shop (Ajijic was no longer the simple village of Everett's youth), the Anglo owner expressed delight that the couple she had heard about, the couple who had honeymooned in Chapala in 1926, had come into her store.

"But we all visualized two *old* people," she said. "We had no idea they would look like the two of *you*!"

*

When Eileen and Everett returned to San Diego in the fall, Eileen began her new life. She had it all planned out. She would do volunteer work, and she would give dinner parties. When one attends three hundred and twenty-five parties a year, it is difficult to "pay back" one's hosts in kind. Eileen knew that the people whose parties she wrote up did not expect her to give a party in return, but she still felt an obligation to entertain some of those people someday. For a number of years she and Everett had invited their family and close friends to a buffet supper in the studio on Christmas Eve, but they had long ago ceased giving small dinner parties *in* their home. For one thing, in those days they were rarely in their home during the early hours of an evening. Now, however, Eileen was ready to start paying back the people she felt they owed.

My parents gave a series of small seated dinners that fall and winter, each for ten people, eight of whom were guests. Eileen had one menu, a gourmet menu, involving chutney chicken. A bachelor friend named Legler Benbough came to their house several times, as he was the chosen escort of several widowed women. Eileen apologized to him for serving him the same meal over and over. He told her that he didn't mind at all.

"It's a very good meal," he said, "and you are the only hostess who ever serves it to me."

After four or five months of entertaining, it began to dawn on Eileen that she and Everett could never pay back the countless people they owed if they only had eight people to dinner at a time. Content to have made a start, she decided they should stop giving dinner parties. They planned to co-host a big bash sometime later with a regal-looking, warm-hearted friend of theirs, Justine Fenton. Justine owned a beautiful house in the country, with space outdoors for hundreds of guests. The three finally did get around to co-hosting that big party, in October of 1982. Meanwhile, in 1977, Eileen sighed with relief as she gave up her series of dinners.

*

In March of 1977 Eileen, in her new role as an "occasional contributor," wrote a long, well-researched article for the *Union* about the Duchess of Windsor. In her article Eileen stressed the

Duchess' Coronado connection. Eileen sent a copy of it to Pat Nixon, along with a letter. The article mentioned a party the Nixons had given for the Windsors at the White House in 1970. Eileen thought the former First Lady might enjoy the story and the reference to her party.

Mrs. Nixon wrote and thanked Eileen for her letter and for sending the article. Then she added, "It is apparent that retirement has not affected your superb writing style!"

That article on the Duchess was the only thing Eileen wrote in 1977. That same year she began her volunteer work, choosing two groups that interested her: the Zoological Society of San Diego and the San Diego Opera Association. The zoo put her on its development committee, and the opera made her a member of its advisory board.

Eileen was particularly fond of the zoo, and she felt flattered some years later when the zoo named a snow leopard after her. Everett said that Eileen and the snow leopard looked like each other, that their faces were similar. He felt there was a definite kinship between the two Eileens.

In 1977 Eileen not only became a volunteer, but she also became a public speaker. That December she gave a talk to a group that she greatly respected, a women's cultural organization in San Diego called the Wednesday Club. Her talk, which was about the club and its members, emphasized events that had taken place during the thirties and the forties. She used as her source material *San Diego Union* society-section pages from those two decades, pages which a librarian had given to her. She brought many of the clippings with her to the meeting and displayed them as part of her talk.

Eileen had agreed to speak to the club when she learned that she could *read* her entire speech. She never spoke extemporaneously to any group. It was strange, but Eileen, who was not afraid to telephone the White House, to ask questions of a First Lady, or even to chat with a queen, could not speak in public before large numbers of people. She would freeze when asked to stand up before an audience and talk. Everett said that on the few occasions when she had tried to say some sentences to a roomful of people, she had turned into a "timid mouse." Those are certainly not the words one would normally use to describe Eileen.

In the paper she read to the Wednesday Club, Eileen proved again that she was a thorough researcher. She had combed through the old pages of the *Union* and had found just the right items that were needed for her talk. Now that she was retired, many of her friends hoped that she would write a book about her experiences as a newspaperwoman. For some reason the idea of writing such a book never appealed to her. She had enjoyed researching her paper, but after immersing herself in the thirties and forties for several weeks, she was ready to start looking forward again.

I believe that Eileen shied away from writing a book about her past because it was not in her nature to look backward. Although she did reminisce occasionally, in her journals and in conversation, she preferred to think about the future. Once in a while someone would interview her. Then she would dutifully recall various incidents from her early life. She was always relieved, though, when the interview was over and she could look ahead again.

Her family often teased her for consistently making herself out to be one year older than she actually was. If she celebrated her seventy-first birthday one day, the following day she would tell people she was seventy-two. She did this unconsciously; she couldn't help herself. She was always looking forward—to the next story, to the next year.

In 1978 the Wednesday Club invited Eileen to become a member. She gladly accepted the invitation. In the next few years she gave several more talks to the club, including one in which she interviewed a beloved hundred-year-old member named Grace Klauber. The two sat on the stage, where Eileen asked pithy questions of her bright centenarian friend, and received pithy answers in reply. The Wednesday Club was a source of pleasure to Eileen from the day she joined, and in her final years it was the source of most of her social life. In fact, the last social event she ever attended was a Wednesday Club tea.

*

In February of 1978 Eileen and Everett went back to Honduras, stopping off in Mexico City and Guatemala on the way. Their friend Justine Fenton and one of their grandsons accompanied them. It was Everett's fourth trip to Copán, and Eileen's third. Again she wrote a travel article for the *Union*, and again Everett illustrated her story.

In 1979 the Museo del Carmen, in San Angel, Mexico City, presented a retrospective exhibition of Everett's paintings. In March of that year one hundred and twenty-five San Diegans flew south to attend the opening of the exhibition. Several dozen Texans joined them. After the three days of festivities in the capital were over, Eileen and Everett prolonged the trip by traveling with some of their friends to several other cities in Mexico. As always, they left Mexico with reluctance. They never crossed the border back into the United States without feeling that their trip had ended too soon.

*

In the summer of 1979 Eileen helped put on another wedding in the studio. That July their older grandson was married in front of the big north window, where his parents had been married twenty-eight years before. The wedding preparations kept Eileen occupied, but a few days after the wedding Everett noticed a strange look in her eye. It was a restless look. It was the look of a woman who wished she could go back to work.

Eileen lasted as a housewife and volunteer for almost two more years. In 1980 she became a member of the advisory board of the library at San Diego State. That year she also started a program of walking. Each day she walked several miles, holding an umbrella over her head, to protect her from the sun. Strangers began to greet her on her walks. She became known in her neighborhood as the "Umbrella Lady." But she still had a restless look. In 1981, the same year that she was asked to join—and did join—the board of the San Diego Historical Society, a friend from the past suddenly made her an offer that she knew she had to accept.

Ever since Eileen's days on the *Journal*, she had maintained a friendship with the reporter Neil Morgan. His lively, anecdotal column about San Diego and San Diegans had been a popular feature in the *Journal*. When the *Journal* folded, he moved over to the *Tribune* and took his column with him. It became even more popular. People all over town aspired to have their names appear in it.

Neil went on contributing to his column even after he became associate editor of the *Tribune*, in 1977, and then editor, in 1981. As editor his main challenge was to keep the *Tribune* from folding. Like other evening papers in the country at that time, it was experiencing a drop in readership. Americans preferred to get their news from television in the evening rather than from a newspaper. Eileen was sure Neil could save the *Tribune* if anyone could. She told her family that Helen Copley knew Neil was an imaginative, creative person, and that Helen was undoubtedly counting on him to dream up some features to attract readers to the paper.

Neil was so imaginative he thought of asking an almost-seventy-five-year-old woman reporter to come out of retirement and join his staff. He offered Eileen the job of writing a weekly social editorial, or essay, or whatever she wanted to call it, for the *Tribune*. Essentially it was to be a commentary on the "changing social patterns" of the community. Eileen's eyes lit up, and she accepted his offer. She knew that a once-a-week editorial would be a snap to write after all those daily columns she had turned out for so many years. She could keep up her volunteer work *and* write for Neil. She was overjoyed.

The first articles Eileen wrote for the *Tribune* that spring had an editorial tone. In fact, she began her very first one, which appeared on March 5, 1981, with the words:

> With the revival today in The Tribune of my so-called "social editorial" which appeared in several San Diego newspapers for nearly 50 years, I am challenged to reflect on changes, as well as constants, in social coverage in San Diego.

For several weeks her articles continued to sound like

editorials, but by mid-April local names had begun to creep into her copy. Each week she would have a theme for her article, but then she would take off and enrich the theme by adding names—the names of San Diegans of the past and present, the names of people that her readers knew. Soon she was writing both an editorial and a social column. It was an irresistible combination—a new art form—and it quickly caught on.

On May 7, for example, Eileen wrote about "laughter" and the fact that the "average American laughs 15 times a day." After talking about laughter for a few paragraphs, she then recalled some amusing incidents that had taken place in San Diego in the past, and she mentioned the names of the San Diego residents who were involved in those incidents.

Neil Morgan had known what he was doing when he offered Eileen a job. More people began to subscribe to the *Tribune*, and, according to their letters to Eileen, one of the reasons why they did was because of her column. Some friends told her that they still subscribed to the *Union*, but that they went to a newsstand and bought the Thursday edition of the *Tribune* each week, so they could read her words. Still others called the *Tribune* to find out if they could subscribe to that paper *just* on Thursdays. They couldn't, but Eileen was pleased to think they had tried.

Neil had another creative idea that spring. He decided that Eileen would be the perfect reporter to send to England that summer to cover the wedding of Prince Charles and Lady Diana Spencer. Neil was the ideal editor for Eileen. They were very much alike. At age seventy-five she found herself working with a person who understood her spirited dedication to hard work and her imaginative approach to a story. Neil knew Eileen wouldn't let him down. Many editors dealing with a woman of her age might have hesitated to give her such a challenging assignment, but Neil had confidence in Eileen. She appreciated his confidence, and she agreed to go to England.

Eileen began to prepare for her trip, but meanwhile she kept writing her weekly articles. In her June 25 editorial/social column, she discussed the "power of light." She wrote of candlelight, moonlight, hearth-fire light. Then she went on to say:

> Historians have given Mrs. Richard Nixon credit for turning the lights back on at the White House after President Lyndon Johnson's era of "frugal lights." The decisions to add floodlights on the mansion at night and to replace early American lighting in the Grand Hallway with shimmering crystal chandeliers were hers.

Eileen mailed that article to Mrs. Nixon, and enclosed a note with it. Four years had passed since they had last written to each other, and Eileen thought Pat Nixon might like to know that she—and her accomplishments—were still remembered. Also Eileen wanted to share the news of her exciting new assignment.

Mrs. Nixon wrote Eileen and thanked her for her kind words, for mentioning "one of my contributions to the White House." She said she was "delighted to be 'put in a good light' by a valued friend!" and she added, "How thrilled you must be with your assignment to cover the royal wedding. You will do a superb job as always!"

With that endorsement, Eileen was ready to tackle England. In the weeks leading up to her departure date, she wrote several articles about the coming wedding, including one in which she discussed the "mystique of monarchy." She talked with San Diegans living in London, and in her column she reported what they had to say about the current mood in their adopted city. She also talked with Mrs. Alfred Bloomingdale of Los Angeles, who would be attending the wedding with her husband. Mrs. Bloomingdale, who was a close friend of Nancy Reagan's, was happy to talk to Eileen. She was very cooperative. Eileen, as usual, was the consummate reporter. After five years of retirement, she was as sharp as ever. She hadn't lost her ability to dig and push—to chase after a story.

On July 2, 1981, the *Tribune* announced that Eileen, accompanied by her husband, would be in London from July 25 through August 1. On June 8 President Ronald Reagan had presented one of Everett's paintings as a gift of state to President José López Portillo of Mexico. Everett had received an invitation to have lunch at the White House. He had regretfully declined, for he knew that in approximately six weeks he would be leaving for London with Eileen. At age eighty, he didn't feel he was up to two big trips in one summer.

*

Eileen and Everett arrived in London four days before the wedding was to take place, and Eileen got right to work. As in Canada, in 1957, her first job was to pick up her credentials. After establishing themselves at their hotel, the Stafford, on St. James' Place, she and Everett walked to the British Government Press Centre to get the credentials. Eileen was glad to have Everett with her on this trip, and in the long run his constant presence at her side proved practical as well as comforting. He became so well known at the Press Centre that the Press Centre Chief bent the rules the day before the wedding and allowed him to assume a temporary, but important, role.

Eileen was supposed to go to the Press Centre at nine a.m. the day of the wedding to pick up the official description of the wedding dress. She was told she could go later if she wished, but nine a.m. was the hour when the closely guarded description would be released. At nine, Eileen pointed out to the Press Chief, she would be hurrying to her assigned window at the Savoy Hotel, where she was to watch the wedding procession. And, she reminded him, after the wedding was over she would have to rush back to her hotel and start writing, in order to make her paper's deadline. She would have no time to pick up the dress description either before or after the wedding. Eileen added that she knew her readers at home would be very disappointed if that dress wasn't described.

She asked the Press Chief if a messenger from her hotel could pick it up for her, but the Press Chief told her that only accredited reporters could obtain the description. Suddenly the Press Chief had an idea on how to resolve the problem: he would accredit Everett and allow *him* to pick up the dress description for Eileen. Over the past few days the Press Chief had gotten to know Everett's face, and he must have liked what he saw, or maybe he was charmed by these two unusual Americans, these senior citizens who were dashing about London like a couple of kids.

Neil Morgan wrote in his July 29 column:

> Our own Eileen Jackson, at 75, wondered if she was up to the crush and competition of covering the royal wedding this morning in London. Tribune readers know by now that she was and is. But she enlisted the aid of a fleet assistant for whom she managed at the last minute to wangle press credentials so that he could run errands for her: her husband, Everett … At 80, he figured to be the senior copyboy covering the wedding.

Three days before the wedding, on July 26—on what Eileen described as a "moody, gray day"—she and Everett walked the route from Buckingham Palace to St. Paul's Cathedral. They were following the rehearsal procession. The rehearsal scene, with its parade of empty coaches and mounted police, was so colorful that, as Eileen said in an article on July 27, "it was hard to realize principals and music were lacking."

In another article that appeared on that date Eileen noted:

> The royal wedding is coming on strong. The heart of London is charged with excitement as everything escalates toward Wednesday, when Prince Charles and Lady Diana will exchange vows. London is … upbeat and sunny, despite overcast, moody skies.

The night before the wedding, Eileen and Everett watched the Hyde Park fireworks display from a window on Park Lane. In her story the next day Eileen said:

> Not even in Elizabethan times and before, when royal weddings were celebrated with fire-spouting dragons and fiery Thames River pageants, have Londoners seen anything quite like last night's

> bachelor party for Prince Charles.
>
> A dazzling fireworks display signaled the end of his single days.
>
> Prince Charles was accompanied to the Hyde Park display by his parents, Queen Elizabeth II and Prince Philip, and by other members of the royal family. After the royal party arrived Prince Charles lighted the first of a nationwide chain of 101 beacons and bonfires.

Eileen remarked that that night there was plenty of music. She wrote:

> The 25-minute show, involving 12,000 fireworks, weighing 2½ tons, was coordinated with music … Four hundred performers in massed bands took part in the fireworks extravaganza.

Eileen sent articles back to the paper, reporting on all these events. Then, on July 29, came the wedding day. It was bright and sunny, just the kind of day everyone had hoped for. In her July 29 article Eileen described the wedding procession on the Strand, a procession complete with principals this time and "orchestrated with music all the way." Included in her story was a long description of the wedding dress. Everett and the kindly British Press Chief had come through.

That night Eileen and Everett attended two gala balls, and the next morning they watched as the clean-up crews of London began to remove the trash that had accumulated along the royal wedding route. The festival was over, but, as Eileen commented after returning home, the afterglow remained. In her August 6 article, written in San Diego, she said:

> Afterglow is one of the most rewarding gifts of a trip, a party or many other special experiences. Frequently it is evoked by the least dramatic phase of the event …
>
> My recent trip to London during royal wedding

> week was rich in experiences. The pageantry … the drama and the fairy-tale quality of it all will remain with me always …
>
> I find myself recalling, again and again, such small pleasures as riding on top of a double-decker bus, where I caught the mood of the city, or looking at a misty view of the great dome of St. Paul's Cathedral from the embankment of the Thames River …
>
> The proud gleaming horses in the wedding procession left a special afterglow with me. I walked with them for four miles (from Buckingham Palace to St. Paul's Cathedral and back), when they were rehearsing for the wedding …
>
> The stars of the wedding—the Prince and Princess of Wales, of course—gave the world its most enduring afterglow. For each spectator, there remains an indelible special image of them. The wave of the Princess' delicate hand … when she passed my window brought her as close to me as her smile. Perhaps, I imagined, she was waving to me.

*

Tom, our daughter, Hildy, and I picked Eileen and Everett up at the airport upon their return from London. At that point they should have felt some jet lag, and probably they did. However, when Eileen heard her eleven-year-old granddaughter mumble that she was getting hungry, Eileen instantly forgot about jet lag.

"Are you hungry, dear?" she said. "I'll fix you some dinner just as soon as we get home!"

I thought to myself that not many seventy-five-year-old grandmothers would have the stamina and drive, much less the talent, to cover a royal wedding in London. I also thought that few would have the energy, after flying six thousand miles, to cook a grandchild's dinner.

My husband and I did not let Eileen cook that dinner when she got home. She wanted to, but we told her that she deserved a rest.

Adelante por Atrás

When Eileen returned home from England that summer, most of her readers showered her with compliments. They thought she'd done a fine job at covering the royal wedding. The Wednesday Club even asked her to give a talk about her experiences in London, which she did in October. But some San Diegans were less enthusiastic. To a minority of readers, the whole idea of covering a royal *anything* was a waste of time. One man wrote in a letter to the editor that he was sick of hearing about royalty, and that if Eileen liked royalty so much she should stay in England.

Eileen was sorry the man felt that way, but she didn't let his criticism bother her. She knew there were people in England as well as in America who thought it was ridiculous to pay so much attention to the royal family. She also knew there were people in San Diego who disliked all social columns, who felt that social columnists were snobs. Those people believed that society columnists like herself were only interested in writing about the rich—or, better still, about the royal rich.

Eileen was not a snob. She was a very friendly person. As Everett had said, her primary interest was people. She could tell you the life story of almost every check-out clerk in the supermarket where she shopped, and on trips to Mexico she conversed with the poorest village women as easily as she did with the society matrons in the cities. She had to admit, though, that she liked to write up glamorous parties, the kind of parties where the hosts spared no expense. She suspected that the majority of her readers liked her to describe such parties. She doubted they really wanted to read about somebody's potluck supper.

Judging from the letters she received, many people who were not social types themselves did enjoy reading about the royal family and about the glamorous events she attended. They told her that her column was fun to read, even if they didn't personally know any of the people who were in it. In a letter to the editor, written while Eileen was still writing for the *Union*, a local woman had said:

> I am a housewife. I am not society-minded, nor am I socially-inclined, but I must tell Eileen Jackson that reading her "Straws in the Wind" each morning in The Union certainly adds a dash of glamour to my otherwise routine day.
>
> Through her eloquent writings I have traveled all over the world, attended social functions in Europe and the Far East …
>
> I have also enjoyed dinner parties before attending the opera or perhaps the ballet. Many times I have danced until dawn at one of the many fancy-dress balls.
>
> All this I have done for the small price of a monthly subscription to your newspaper. Thank you very much.

Needless to say, Eileen always liked hearing from good-natured readers like that woman. They made up for the grumpy individuals who derided her column.

*

The years from 1981 to 1992 were happy, productive ones for Eileen and Everett. Looking back now, I realize that those were my parents' Golden Years, the Golden Years everybody talks about and hopes to enjoy. Eileen and Everett were old, but they didn't feel it or act it. Except for a few days in 1986 when Everett's blood pressure went sky-high, their health was good.

For those eleven years they lived the kind of life one dreams of living in one's old age.

Neil Morgan had done Eileen an enormous favor when he invited her to come out of retirement and write for the *Tribune*. She found it easy to produce a weekly column, and she liked being back in the thick of things.

Everett was busy, too. In 1981 he began writing books. He wrote and illustrated four in all. They were memoirs about his days in Mexico in the twenties, about his later trips to Mexico, Guatemala, and Honduras, and about his childhood and youth in Texas. The first, which was published in 1985, was a lyrical account of his four years in Mexico in the 1920s, and it was also a loving tribute to his bride, Eileen.

The Texas A&M University Press published two of Everett's books, and that gave Eileen and Everett an added excuse to visit Texas. During the eighties they made three trips to Texas, but the first two had nothing to do with books. In the fall of 1981 the Jackson family held a reunion in Everett's hometown of Mexia. Everett and one of his sisters represented the older generation at the gathering. Eileen wrote a column about the reunion in which she said:

> Yes, YOU CAN go home again, but home won't be the same. For better or worse, the experience will be rich in memories and comparisons …
>
> Driving … through Mexia, sentimental Everett noted sadly that the fountain that used to be in the town center had vanished. His sister reminded him that it had not been a decorative fountain but just a practical horse-watering trough.

Everett enjoyed seeing Mexia again, even without its "fountain," and he enjoyed seeing his relatives. But the highlight of the trip for him was the visit to the Den, the little cottage on the Jackson acreage near Palestine, Texas, where he and Eileen had lived after their return from Mexico in 1926. A deserted shack in 1981, the Hunter's Den now housed wild life rather than human beings, but it was still a family shrine. Everett loved that spot almost more than he loved Mexico, and Eileen understood his feelings.

*

In December of 1981 Eileen became a member of The National Society of The Colonial Dames of America. All her life she had known that her Morse great-grandfather was from New England, and that his forefathers (and therefore, hers) had settled in that region "a long time ago." For many years Eileen was too busy herself to take much interest in her ancestors and their accomplishments. When she was in her seventies, however, a chance remark on her part, and a friend's response, caused her to rethink the ancestor business.

One day when she was talking with some friends, one of them mentioned the name of Aaron Burr, the man who had killed Alexander Hamilton in a duel. Eileen laughingly commented that her mother had told her that the notorious Aaron Burr was one of her ancestors.

"If you're related to *him*," the friend said, "and if you can prove it, then you should be in the Colonial Dames. You really ought to look into this!"

Curious now about her Puritan forebears, Eileen got a genealogist to help her with her paper-work. A year or so later, on December 7, 1981, the Colonial Dames accepted her as a member. In the end she did not research her possible Aaron Burr connection. She followed other leads and found some ancestors on her family tree who she felt were more presentable, ancestors who, as far as she knew, had never killed anyone in a duel.

Eileen settled into the Colonial Dames with as much pleasure as she had settled into the Wednesday Club. She decided that she, like her mother before her, was fated to become a late-blooming, dedicated club woman.

*

In October of 1982 Eileen and Everett went back to Texas, first to Texas A&M. For three days Everett shared honors with two other artists who had attended A&M: E. M. ("Buck") Schiwetz and James H. Johnson. Everett had known Buck Schiwetz sixty-one years before, when they had worked together making illustrations for the 1921 Texas A&M yearbook.

After that part of the trip was over, Eileen and Everett continued on to Houston, where Everett celebrated his eighty-second birthday. He was glad to be in Texas for that occasion, surrounded by his numerous, devoted Texas kin.

*

In the winter of 1983 Eileen had something special to write about, for that February Queen Elizabeth and Prince Philip came to San Diego. Before their arrival Eileen wrote two articles on the subject of royalty. In her January 27 column she reminisced about her experiences in 1957, when she covered the royal couple's visit to Canada and the United States. In her February 17 column she wrote about the two Princes of Wales who had visited San Diego, one in 1920, the other in 1974. Then on February 26, the day the royal yacht, Britannia, sailed into San Diego Bay, Eileen reminded her readers that when she was in Ottawa twenty-six years before, she had invited Prince Philip to come to California and to bring the Queen. In Eileen's February 26 article she said:

> His Royal Highness Prince Philip, the Duke of Edinburgh, keeps his word even if it takes him 26 years to get around to it.
>
> On Oct. 12, 1957, at a press reception at Government House in Ottawa, I lightheartedly invited him and Queen Elizabeth II to come to California.
>
> He told me with enthusiasm that … he thought California was a "great idea." … On July 28, 1981, when covering phases of the wedding of Lady Diana and the Prince of Wales, I brought up the prospect of the visit to Michael Shea, handsome, graying press representative of the queen.

> He asked me what Prince Philip had said in 1957. I told him, and he assured me: "If he said they're coming, then they are."
>
> ... Today, Queen Elizabeth and Prince Philip are here, and Shea is with them ...

Eileen was one of three *Tribune* reporters assigned to cover the royal visit. She had an easy time of it, for by then she had become a kind of queen, herself, and queens are spared real drudgery. She was asked to cover Queen Elizabeth's stop at the San Diego Art Museum, and nothing else. Even Eileen's instruction sheet revealed a deference to her status. Below the paragraph which began, "A press briefing will be held 3 p.m. Friday at the Holiday Inn," was written, in red ink, "Eileen need not attend press briefing."

Eileen seemed to enjoy her easy assignment, and she wrote a nice piece about the reception at the museum. If she missed the hustle and bustle of some of her previous assignments, she didn't say so. She told her friends she was just happy that the Prince had finally kept his promise, and had come with the Queen to California.

*

In May of 1983 Eileen and Everett traveled back to the Copper Canyon, in Mexico—back to the Tarahumara Indians. Again Eileen wrote an article about those intriguing people, and again Everett made a sketch to illustrate her story. With them on the trip were some of their favorite camping friends, three of whom were former professors at San Diego State. In her article Eileen said:

> This time I gained new insight on the Tarahumara Indians through my traveling "textbook"—four professors emeriti from San Diego State University. They were Dr. Spencer Rogers, research anthropologist ... Dr. Orrin Klapp, sociologist and author; John Dirks,

> sculptor, and my husband, a painter, who has lived and traveled in Mexico over a period of 60 years.

With artists', poets', and scholars' eyes, these interesting men and their equally interesting wives absorbed the grandeur of the Copper Canyon. But the party also included a real-estate broker, and even he, Eileen wrote, "evaluated Copper Canyon in aesthetic, not commercial terms."

While in that area, the group visited a Tarahumara cave. Eileen noted and then wrote about the Tarahumara women's "typical colorful cotton blouses and voluminous skirts." Once again she was describing women's wear.

In July of 1983 some of the same people who had gone with Eileen and Everett to the Copper Canyon now joined them on a trip to Laguna Hanson, in Baja California. This time the lake was full. It looked the way it had in 1938 and 1939. In her article of August 4, 1983, Eileen wrote:

> ADELANTE POR ATRAS (advance backward) seems to define the vacation travel routes my family and friends favor in Mexico.
>
> Joined by compatible *companeros*, we tend to seek new experiences, or to refresh old ones, by going back to familiar haunts where the pace of the past still persists.
>
> This July my husband and I returned to the idyllic pine-clad high plateau country of the Sierra de Juarez, northern Baja California. Our destination was the highland's brilliant gem, Laguna Hanson, a shining blue lake at 5,400 feet elevation … which attracted us first in the … '30's before the area was a Mexican national park.
>
> The last time we were in this forest of lofty ponderosa pines was in 1961. The 1958 Power Wagon Dodge four-wheel-drive truck which served as our rugged transportation then, faithfully lunged us in again last month over roads which members of our party described as everything from

> "ornery" to "horrendous."
>
> ... the shallow lake often is dry. It now is full and sparkling blue (one mile long and a half-mile wide), mirroring the incredibly beautiful pine-forested shoreline.

The friends enjoyed the days they spent in that peaceful place, although they all deplored the graffiti that marred some of the large granite boulders surrounding the lake. Apparently Laguna Hanson had finally become part of the modern world. Everett drew a sketch of those boulders and the lake, to illustrate Eileen's article, but in his drawing he edited out the graffiti.

The following year, in March of 1984, the Laguna Hanson campers joined a group of San Diego Art Museum members on a trip to Costa Rica. Eileen and Everett were happy to return to the country where they had made so many friends in 1962. Their travels in the nineteen-eighties all seemed to be examples of *adelante por atrás*.

*

In the spring of 1985 Everett's first book came out, and on March 29 Eileen and Everett attended what Eileen referred to as an "autograph extravaganza" in Austin, Texas. The Governor of Texas had proclaimed that day "Frank Wardlaw Day," in honor of the man who had organized the University of Texas Press in 1950 and the Texas A&M University Press in 1974. Everett's book and the books of two other authors were the first ones in a new "Wardlaw series." The book-signing party, which included a buffet dinner after the autographing was done, was a lively event. Many of Everett's Texas relatives were present, and also on hand, as Eileen was quick to discover, was Liz Carpenter, Lady Bird Johnson's staff director when Mrs. Johnson was the nation's First Lady.

In her April 18 column Eileen described both the book-signing party and the trip she and Everett took afterwards. Their San Diego friends John and Ruth Dirks had accompanied them to Austin. Over the years those two had camped with

Eileen and Everett in Baja California, and had traveled with them to the Copper Canyon and to Costa Rica. Now Everett took them to the Den.

They drove past miles of wildflowers on their way to Palestine, Texas. Texas was showing off for them that spring. Eileen reported that the wildflowers, the "dazzling waves of ubiquitous bluebonnets and scarlet Indian paintbrush," were intoxicating in their beauty.

John and Ruth understood the lure of the Den when Everett showed it to them. For many years they had heard about that little house and the wild acreage surrounding it. They spent several hours exploring the property with Eileen and Everett and some of Everett's relatives. The day at the Den was as memorable as the book-signing party had been.

My parents never returned to Texas after that visit. They always thought they might. They always hoped they would. But at least their last view of Texas was a glorious one, and they were in good spirits as they left. It was impossible to feel sad when all the fields in the state were ablaze with flowers.

*

In July of 1985 Eileen and Everett drove their camper across the border for the last time. They didn't know that that would be their final camping trip in Mexico. It was, in fact, a trip filled with fun and adventure. Even the problems they had with the car made them laugh. Eileen wrote a fine account of the trip for the paper. Reading her words today, those who were there start to grin as they recall the events she described. She was writing about the "end of an era," but since she didn't know it, her story comes across as upbeat and amusing—which is just the way she would want it. In her article entitled "Rough ride was worth it on Baja trip" she wrote:

> Wander off the main roads and you can lose yourself and find a relaxed change of pace. Sometimes it's tough getting to a rustic easy street, but it's usually worth the rough ride.

Recently, our party of six men and two women, seeking escape for a few days from a computerized world, returned again to Baja California, not deterred by reports of problems at and below the border. Our group was conditioned to the trials and rewards of such an excursion as we headed south toward a favorite seaside setting. It is in a remote area of Northern Baja that is given little mention in guidebooks.

Our party of eight included a doctor, a lawyer, a merchant chief, a painter, a poet, a sculptor and two scribes. As it turned out, we also needed a good automobile mechanic. The trip, as far as my husband and I were concerned, added another chapter to the saga of our 1958 Power Wagon Dodge four-wheel-drive truck, which has carried us for 27 years over 56,611 Mexican miles.

This time the truck leaped to the challenge, as if to urge us to remember its best past performances and to forget about the time its leaking oil line caused a delay in Ciudad Constitución, 130 miles north of La Paz, and the year its dust-filled carburetor held us up at Maneadero, south of Ensenada …

The truck's most dramatic mishap took place in July 1979 when our grandson, W. D. (Michael) Waterman drove it in Baja. We received a shocking message from Punta Cabras, south of our recent encampment, advising us that the camper had broken in half on a hilly remote road. Two "bounce-aways" and the rails of the frame had broken, buckling the camper. Twelve Mexicans came to his aid, and the letter's postscript assured us: "All is weld that ends weld."

Each of these experiences caused my husband to declare vehemently: "I'm going to get rid of this darn truck."

On our recent trip, we learned that you

sometimes can get more mechanical help than you need in Mexico ... En route south, all went well until we stopped for gasoline at the Pemex station in Ensenada on the Transpeninsular Highway I ...

This time our grandson, Michael, again was at the wheel. As he headed for the gas pump, he was alarmed when the truck brakes failed. Shifting the truck into reverse, he averted a collision with the automobile in front of him. Our other grandson, Dr. Stephen H. Waterman, and John Freeman, of The Tribune sports department, rushed to a nearby garage for help, returning with a young grease-stained mechanic. The young man confirmed what a member of our group, Richard Rogers, had suspected—the hydraulic brake line had broken, causing the brake fluid to leak out. The mechanic said he needed to seek repair material and would return soon. When his absence extended more than an hour, our flexible companions pondered the possibility of an overnight stay in Ensenada or an altogether thwarted trip. As I surveyed our camper piled high with turbo boards for surfing, tents, cots, fishing rods, bed rolls and food for hearty appetites, my optimism waned.

When the Ensenada mechanic's return became even more uncertain, our lawyer grandson, Michael, with built-in practicality, rushed to find another truck expert. Just as our replacement help was crawling underneath the truck, the first willing—but tardy—mechanic returned, and we faced the rare, awkward experience of two competing workers under our vehicle at the same time.

When both were stifled by a lack of the proper tools for the job, our sculptor companion, John Dirks, produced from his van a 40-piece socket wrench set. The eyes of the competitors brightened. However, not one piece would fit. This time both

> young helpers fled. They eventually returned with time-worn tools and performed a successful mechanical duet. My husband paid the rivals the modest sum they asked, and we all pulled out deciding that two heads were better than one.

Eileen continued her article, describing the road that led to the sea from the highway south of Santo Tomás:

> The road was in fair condition, but our lurching truck made it seem like a washboard for the 20 miles to the serene shore. The road, in fact, was so rough at times that those who took turns driving had to hold on to the gearshift lever to keep the transmission from joggling into neutral, as it did on several occasions.
>
> … As we dipped toward the seashore, we came to a sign arched over the road reading: "Rancho Ganadero—San Juan de Las Pulgas (Cattle Ranch—St. John of the Fleas)." Here we surveyed a wide vista of wheat and oat fields, leading to sharply eroded cliffs high above a lonely beach. A closer look revealed a sparkling sea with frothy surf and picturesque coves. In this restful magic retreat, untouched by progress, we established camp.

Eileen wrote that the members of their group swam, surfed and fished, although "the fishing was not as rewarding as on other occasions." Perhaps because of the poor fishing conditions, they had the campsite to themselves. She added:

> Vista viewing proved our most rewarding entertainment. It's easy to get high on sunsets at this camp …
>
> Each night at sunset, we sat on a bluff, breathing clean air as we surveyed in turn the moving seascape and the calm landscape of serene fields and low mountains backed by lofty ones.

> We brought to camp several of the comforts of home, and some of the supply items suggested for off-road Baja trips by the Automobile Club of Southern California …
>
> The list didn't mention one emergency item that came in handy in our camp one night—a candle brought into camp by Ruth Dirks. When she learned that John Freeman was observing his birthday in camp, she produced the fat, white candle and mounted it in a cupcake for him. His companions sang the Mexican birthday song, "Las Mañanitas."
>
> Breaking camp revealed again that most of us take too much stuff with us on such trips, including an oversupply of food. We learned again that breaking camp can be sad in any country.
>
> The old truck lunged back over the road reluctantly, seemingly as loathe to leave as its passengers. Despite the fact that it competed successfully on the return trip with younger vehicles, its owner again declared: "I'm going to get rid of this darned truck."

That November the old truck made it to one last Thanksgiving camp, but the camp was not in Mexico. Some of Eileen and Everett's older camping companions had developed a fear of Mexico. The group went to a California desert instead.

The truck barely made it home from that trip. Climbing the mountain pass was almost too much for it. Eileen agreed with Everett that their truck was ready to retire. A few months later they sold it, for a very small sum, to a Mexican. The new owner told Everett that the truck's problems didn't bother him at all. He said he was a mechanic, and that he was looking forward to working on his new possession.

Honors and Celebrations

On April 15, 1986, Eileen celebrated her eightieth birthday, and six hundred of her friends celebrated it with her. A committee of women headed by one of Everett's favorite former art students had been working for weeks planning the luncheon event.

Everett had always deplored the fact that his former student Betty Marshall Hubbard had chosen to chair balls and other large functions rather than stick to her art. "She's gone the chairwoman route," he said, "which is a pity, because she was such a good artist—one of the best students I ever had." Everett had to admit, though, that Betty's organizational skills had created a birthday party that was a work of art.

The luncheon took place in the ballroom of San Diego's Grant Hotel. Eileen's editor, Neil Morgan, served as the master of ceremonies, and "her people," all those people she had written about for so many years, formed a sea of birthday-party guests. Eileen noticed, to her surprise, that many men were present, and that a number of her Tijuana friends had crossed the border to attend her party.

After George Sorenson, longtime drummer in the Mission Hills String Quartet, had rolled his drums, Howard Chernoff led that famed musical group in "Happy Birthday." Then Everett took over the mike and sang "Las Mañanitas" to Eileen. It was a lovefest from beginning to end. Eileen said later that as she looked down on the crowd from her seat at the elevated head table, she thought to herself: What a huge amount of people! And

I bet I've written up the wedding of almost every person here!

*

That summer Neil Morgan again offered Eileen a major assignment. She was thrilled, and flattered beyond measure. Neil wanted to send her and Everett to London, so she could cover the wedding of Prince Andrew and Sarah Ferguson. Eileen accepted the assignment and excitedly began preparing for the trip.

At eighty, Eileen was still full of energy. Unfortunately Everett, at eighty-five, was not. He had excelled in London as a fleet-footed "copyboy" when he was eighty, but now, as he approached his eighty-sixth birthday, he was slowing down.

Eileen assured him that he was not slowing down. She told him that if he would just think positively, he would love the idea of going back to London. Even when Eileen heard that she would have to attend an important press briefing right after her arrival, she was unfazed. Tom and I reminded her that one needed at least a day to recover from jet lag after a flight from California to England. The thought of Eileen getting off the plane and going straight to a press briefing horrified us.

But it didn't horrify Eileen. Her energy level was always astounding. Out of all her immediate family, only one of her grandsons possesses that same kind of energy. The rest of us are made of weaker stuff. Eileen, who was so generous and kind, had one failing when it came to understanding other people: she honestly believed that everyone was as energetic as herself. That blind spot of hers sometimes caused misunderstandings to occur within our family. As a result of her inability to comprehend what Everett was trying to tell her that summer, she kept making plans for the July trip.

The week before they were to leave, Everett became very ill. The doctor who examined him (his physician and friend Merl Ledford) found that Everett's blood pressure had soared to an astonishing height. When Eileen asked hopefully if Everett would be able to leave for London in a week, Merl shook his head. Everett had to rest and take some medication. Merl wanted to observe him over the next few weeks.

Suddenly Eileen understood, and she quickly shifted gears. "Of course we mustn't go. I'll call my editor right away."

Eileen wouldn't think of traveling to London without Everett even if he were well, and she certainly wouldn't think of leaving him when he was sick. She knew his health was far more important than a royal wedding.

She had been ready and eager to take on that assignment. She had wanted to prove that, at eighty, she could still hustle with the best of them, that she could still chase down a story and maybe even scoop a reporter or two. But she gave in gracefully.

From her office at home she wrote three long articles about the coming wedding and about the Prince and his bride-to-be. One of her articles began, "Royal fever is rising again in London." Reading her words, one can easily imagine the mood in that city as the big day approached.

The articles she wrote were so vivid and so full of information that a woman came up to her at a party a few weeks later and congratulated her on her coverage of Andrew and Fergie's wedding. "Aren't you glad you could go to London twice, for *both* those weddings?" the woman said.

Because they stayed home, Eileen and Everett celebrated their sixtieth wedding anniversary that July at a quiet party in San Diego rather than in London. Everett, to his embarrassment, recovered rapidly after he learned that he didn't have to go to England. On July 23 he and Eileen watched the royal wedding on TV. By then Everett's blood pressure had dropped way down, and he was feeling fine again.

*

Eileen continued writing her weekly column for four more years. She wrote about weddings, anniversaries, graduations, parties, and trips. She still began each article with a theme, and then took off from there. As the years passed, she wrote up more and more weddings. Brides—and their mothers—loved her long, detailed, traditional write-ups. Old-time San Diegans felt comfortable reading her column, for it always contained the names of people they knew. But she was quick to add the names of newcomers, too. Eileen had a good time during those four years. Even though she and Everett stayed close to home, they lived full lives, painting, writing, going to parties, and giving them.

On Everett's eightieth birthday, in 1980, he had promised to give Howard Chernoff a party when *he* reached eighty. In December of 1987 that day arrived. Since some of Howard's friends were too infirm to make it down the steps at the House of the Coyote's Song, the party was held at Tom's and my house. It was an elegant affair. Eileen and Everett had the dinner catered, and one of the guests insisted on supplying the flowers. She must have bought out the florist, for floral arrangements were everywhere—on the buffet table, the dining tables, the piano. Tom and I hadn't realized that our home could look so festive. Howard was very pleased with his birthday party. At the end of the evening he promised to give Everett a ninetieth birthday party in three years' time.

*

In the past, Eileen and Everett had received recognition for their achievements, but now the honors began to pour in at a faster pace. Also, their friends used the excuse of birthdays and anniversaries to fete them.

On July 22, 1988, the day after my parents' sixty-second wedding anniversary, they were the honored couple at the San Diego Mission de Alcalá's annual summer dinner dance. As always, the party took place in the mission courtyard under the stars. Some years earlier Everett had sketched that first California mission for one of the mission dances. His drawing was printed on the invitation that year, and it was printed on the dance invitations for many years afterwards. Earlier he had also donated one of his paintings to the mission, a painting he had made of a two-foot-high, antique carved Spanish cross that a friend had given to him back in the thirties. While Everett was providing the mission with his art work, Eileen was writing up the annual dinner dances. They both felt very close to the mission and to its pastor, Monsignor I. Brent Eagen.

During the program at the 1988 party, Monsignor Eagen told the crowd of over five hundred guests that Everett was the "mission's artist" and that Eileen was the "mission's scribe." In addition he announced that they had just celebrated their sixty-second wedding anniversary. Then, to Eileen and Everett's great surprise, he presented them with a framed Papal blessing, which he had obtained for them while visiting Rome a short while before.

They were deeply touched. As they stepped up to receive the large framed blessing, with its picture of the Pope, the crowd gave them a standing ovation. Eileen and Everett took the Papal blessing home and put it in the studio in a place of honor, on the wall right above that antique Spanish cross that Everett had painted for the mission.

*

The honors kept coming; the celebrations continued. That October Justine Fenton gave a gigantic birthday party for Everett at her country home. She felt the date was special: Everett was eighty-eight on October 8, 1988. "We are celebrating," she said, "eighty-eight years of Everett!"

In May of 1990 Eileen and Everett shared alumni-of-the-year honors at a San Diego State awards dinner. Five months later Howard Chernoff gave Everett his promised ninetieth birthday party. Evelyn Klapp, one of my parents' closest friends, wrote a poem commemorating the occasion. It began, "I come to praise the Venerable one …" Everett, feeling venerable but frisky that night, promised that in seven years he would give Howard a party.

In November of 1990 Eileen wrote her last column for the *Tribune*. At eighty-four, she felt it was time to take a rest, or perhaps she felt it was time for Everett to take one. But she and Everett didn't stop going to parties; they just went to fewer than before.

Again, people asked Eileen if she was going to write a book.

"Oh, no," she said, "Everett is writing them now." Everett's second book had come out in 1987, and he was then working on his third.

Eileen said in an interview that upon retirement she was "going to learn the family business." That comment fascinated the rest of us in the family. We weren't sure just what the "family business" was. Eileen wasn't sure either, so, since no one seemed to know, she never had to learn it.

She kept busy, though, in other ways. Taking care of Everett took up much of her time. His mind was as sharp as it had ever been, but he tired easily. As they began to stay home more often, Eileen again turned into a gourmet cook. She also kept up her interest in the zoo and in the San Diego Historical Society, and she never missed a Wednesday Club or Colonial Dames meeting.

Then, in 1991, groups began to honor Eileen and Everett again. "That's what happens when you grow old," Everett said. "People start to honor you."

In March of 1991 Eileen was chosen to ride in San Diego's Saint Patrick's Day parade as "Woman of the Year." She rode in an open car with Everett and several dignitaries. She wore a Kelly-green coat and looked about forty years old at the most.

Her family members were sitting in a special section of the bleachers at a certain point along the route. When the car reached that point, Eileen and Everett were allowed to get out and join their family. As Eileen stepped out of the car, a member of the County Board of Supervisors, who was sitting next to me, turned to me and said, "Did you know that Eileen Jackson was born in 1906? Can you believe it? And she's *beautiful*!"

I smiled and told him that yes, I did know it, for I was her daughter.

"Well, she doesn't look anywhere near her age," he said. "The years have certainly treated her kindly."

Eileen did look especially beautiful that day, and incredibly young. Everett was proud that he was her escort, but he still could be a tease. When someone asked him how come he got to ride in that car when he wasn't Irish, he replied, "I got to ride in it as a reward for having lived for nearly sixty-five years with an Irishwoman!"

In June it was Everett's turn: San Diego State named a campus art gallery after him, and San Diego State University Press published his third book. In July Justine gave a party at her ranch to celebrate Eileen and Everett's sixty-fifth wedding anniversary.

As my parents grew older, they were honored and feted to an extraordinary degree. They had given a great deal to their community, and their community showed its appreciation over and over again. No one could say that those two were unloved or unnoticed during their final years.

*

In January of 1992 the first indication that the Golden Years might be ending occurred. Everett developed pneumonia twice that month, and twice had to be rushed to the hospital. After the second time, tests were done which explained why he kept getting pneumonia: he had multiple myeloma, a cancer of the bone marrow. From then on, his life revolved around two fine men—Doctors William Stanton and Howard Williams.

When Everett went into the hospital, Eileen's brother, Bill, came to stay with her. She had always counted on him to be there if she needed him, and he had never let her down.

That summer Eileen and Everett were honored again. At an impressive luncheon ceremony the San Diego Rotary Club named them "Mr. and Mrs. San Diego." Governor Wilson was unable to leave Sacramento to present the award, so his attractive, talented wife, Gayle, filled in for him. She did a stellar job, and as part of her presentation she even sang a song. The club had never before named a "Mrs. San Diego." Just as Eileen had been the first girl editor of her high-school paper, now she was leading the way as the first "Mrs. San Diego."

Everett continued to visit his doctors throughout 1993. However, he felt well enough to enjoy a triumph in December of that year, when San Diego State published his fourth book.

That same December Eileen gave her family a scare. At dusk on Christmas Eve she tripped and fell while feeding the doves in her upper patio. The doves were Everett's special friends. For years he had enticed them into his garden with birdseed, but now he lacked the strength to climb the stairs each day and feed them. Eileen, unable to stand after her fall, and bleeding heavily from a deep cut over her eye, managed to crawl to the still open door and call for help. Everett couldn't lift her, so he alerted Tom and me. Tom hurried to Eileen and Everett's house, and was soon joined by their physician grandson, Steve.

Tom remained with Everett while Steve took Eileen to two emergency rooms. The first one was extremely crowded. Eileen was told that her head wound and wrist pain were not "life threatening," so she would have to wait her turn. Anticipating at least a two-hour wait, her enterprising grandson remembered a new hospital in town that was rarely crowded, and he took Eileen there. She was the only patient in that emergency room. The X-rays revealed that her wrist was not broken, but the doctor sewed up the cut over her eye with eleven stitches and then put a big bandage over the stitches.

"What a shame it is that you have to be here," Eileen said to the young doctor. "It's terrible that you have to work on Christmas Eve."

"Oh, that's all right, Mrs. Jackson," the doctor said. "I don't mind; I'm Jewish."

The next day our family convened at Eileen and Everett's house for a Christmas picnic of turkey sandwiches and such. We couldn't get Eileen to sit down. She insisted on serving the food and rushing about the room, to make sure everyone had enough to eat.

Staring at the big white bandage over her eye, her grandson Michael said to Tom and me, "Don't you think Eileen looks more Irish than usual today?"

"Yes, definitely," said Tom. "She looks as though she's just been through The Troubles!"

By then Eileen had accepted the fact that the Golden Years were over, but her spirit was unbroken. "Bloody but unbowed," as the poem says, she was ready to take on whatever the future had to offer.

Last Years

Eileen liked stories to have happy endings, but she was a realist. She knew that the future she and Everett faced didn't look too promising. Eileen and Everett's last years were difficult simply because they had grown so old. But the slide was gradual. They enjoyed some pleasures still. Their social world had become much smaller, but people did not forget them. They still received countless invitations to parties, most of which they had to regret. Eileen was happy to be invited to the parties; Everett was happy that he didn't have to go to them.

Occasionally they did go out, if someone else could do the driving. In the fall of 1994 Everett was too sick to take his driver's test, so he had to let his license expire. The previous year he had had better luck. When he took the exam in 1993, he flunked the eye test. The examiner told him he would have to see a doctor about his eyes before he could renew his license. Upon returning home, Everett studied his glasses, walked over to the kitchen sink, and washed them. Then he went back to the DMV, and passed the eye test. He drove for another year with those glasses, always careful to keep them clean.

By the end of 1994, however, Eileen was doing the driving. But she only drove in the daytime; she was afraid to drive at night. For many months she made a daily run to the nearby supermarket. She explained that she shopped every day so that her grocery bags would be light and therefore easy to carry down the forty-six steps to the house's lower kitchen. Tom and I suspected that she had a second reason for going so often. We felt she enjoyed the sociability at the store. She admitted that she liked talking to all those nice clerks and learning about their lives.

Eileen took good care of Everett until she developed some serious health problems herself. At that point she had to give up driving. Her family found two caretakers to buy the groceries and to run the house.

Everett died in the hospital on March 4, 1995. A few weeks earlier, he and Eileen had both been in the same hospital at the same time. "This is carrying married togetherness too far!" one of their nurses had teased.

Because Eileen was recovering from a major operation during Everett's last days, she was at home when he slipped away. She and Everett had been a team for so long, and such a successful, loving team, that it was hard to believe one of them was gone. That July they would have been married sixty-nine years.

*

Eileen's world grew even smaller after that. She lived in the House of the Coyote's Song with the caretakers. Although she missed Everett, she was not lonely, for her close friends were never far away. Some drove her to the Wednesday Club each week. Some brought her fresh fruit and vegetables from their gardens. An angel of a neighbor, Elma Forshey, baked her cookies. Three thoughtful men kept her rooms filled with flowers: Tom Sefton, a banker in his seventies, whom Eileen still called "Tommy" because she had known him when he was a boy; Burl Stiff, the social columnist on the *Union*; and Tony Anewalt, who was Eileen's honorary son. Tony's mother had played the piano in the Mission Hills String Quartet and was a good friend of Eileen and Everett's. When she died, Tony asked Eileen if she would please be his mother from then on. Those three men sent Eileen azaleas, orchid plants, and beautiful mixed bouquets.

By that time Eileen had also acquired another honorary son, named Ulad Marsh, and two honorary daughters, Mary Fadem and Joan Jencks. My mother was amused at the way her family kept growing. "It keeps getting bigger!" she said. "I now have two sons, *three* daughters, four grandchildren and ten great-grandchildren. Pretty good, for a woman who started out thinking she only wanted to be a newspaper reporter!"

The telephone played an important part in Eileen's life after Everett was gone. It was her link to the outer world, and she used it almost as much as she had when she was writing a column. In 1995 and 1996, however, most of the people she called were shut-ins. One was Howard Chernoff. Another was a former vocalist and pianist in the inimitable Quartet, a spirited lady in her nineties named Augusta Starkey. Eileen was very fond of Augusta and made a ritual of phoning her every day.

Eileen's longtime friend Myrle Cavell was partially confined to her home by then, so those two also kept in touch by telephone. Other people used the phone to check in with Eileen. Audrey Geisel, Ted Geisel's widow, often called. Ted (Dr. Seuss) and Everett had thoroughly enjoyed each other, and now their widows talked on the phone about how much they missed "those two dear boys." Audrey's calls were a great comfort to Eileen.

In October of 1995 Eileen attended a ceremony in the beautiful Victorian garden of her friends Arthur and Betty Austin. She and seven men were honored that day by their alma mater San Diego High.

One month later, in November, Eileen lost her brother, Bill. His illness had come on suddenly. After that, her once formidable memory began to fail. But it failed in an unusual way. Although she gradually forgot many of the people and incidents from her past, she was well grounded in the present. She not only knew everyone who was part of her present life, but she also proved capable of meeting and remembering new people. Of those who were gone, she remembered Everett and his parents, her brother, and her own parents, and also Lowell Houser, Max Miller, President Roosevelt, and Pat Nixon. As for past events, she could recall some of her favorite newspaper assignments and her horse-and-buggy accident in Ramona, but that was about it.

Her loss of memory didn't seem to worry her. She still had her pleasures, and high on the list were the San Diego Padres. Ever since the time when Eileen had put on the benefit ball game for the Y, she had been a Padres fan. Now, during her last years, Padres baseball had become her passion. She religiously watched the games on TV and listened to them on the radio. Gradually she began to know the names of the players, and she could tell you what positions they played. By the summer of 1996 she had forgotten the names of most of San Diego's social figures, but she knew the names of almost all the Padres.

At a low moment one night, when her chest pains were severe, and when the family was debating whether to call the paramedics, Eileen, in a frenzy, cried out, "Call Tony Gwynn!"

Later, after she was her normal self again, someone reminded her of her frantic request that night. She laughed and said, "I doubt he could have helped."

"Oh, I don't know," one of her grandsons replied. "Tony's pretty talented."

Eileen had a small group of friends whom she telephoned after each game, to report the score. One kindly friend (Phil Klauber, an elderly man, but younger than she) told her that she could call him up to midnight about the Padres, but he asked that she call him only when they won.

*

Another source of pleasure to Eileen during her final years was the Lawrence Welk Show on TV. When she and Everett first began watching it, in 1992, she said to her family, "I used to know some people who wouldn't go to a party the night that show was on TV. They were very prominent people in town, and I always thought, How corny! But now I like it, too. I guess I'm corny now!"

Eileen enjoyed the show because it was upbeat, like her columns. "There's no crime on it," she explained, "and those dancers are so cute, and that Irish tenor is wonderful!"

Tom, Hildy, Joan Jencks and I took Eileen to the Lawrence Welk Christmas program in Escondido in 1995. Her eyes sparkled as she watched and applauded the show. After it was over, Joe Feeney, the Irish tenor, signed her program and told her that her maiden name of Eileen Dwyer was "the most Irish name I've ever heard!"

*

Eileen managed to have some fun during the last year of her life. In between bouts of illness she attended the Wednesday Club meetings and teas. In February she went to the Charity Ball, as Justine Fenton's guest. In recent years she had had to skip that ball because of Everett's health. She had covered it throughout her career—and what's more, she remembered covering it.

In the first week of April she visited Myrle Cavell. They had known each other since 1929, and in spite of Eileen's faulty memory, they had many things to say. They both agreed that seeing each other was better than talking on the phone.

On April 15 Eileen and Stanford Steinbeck, a man she always called her "twin," celebrated their ninetieth birthdays together, at a luncheon for twenty people that three of their friends gave for them. On the Fourth of July Eileen attended a large party at Justine's ranch, an event co-hosted by Justine and the Arthur Austins. My mother sat in the place of honor at the ranch and was the star of the party. Hundreds of people came up to her to say hello. She knew their faces even if she couldn't remember their names. She greeted every one of them with a smile.

Later that summer the Padres honored her. Her next-door neighbor, Ann Bass, had come up with the idea of asking the Padres management to recognize Eileen. Ann made some phone calls, and her efforts were successful. Toward the end of July Eileen received a charming letter from Larry Lucchino, President and Chief Executive Officer of the Padres. In his letter he said:

> Dear Ms. Jackson,
>
> We have come to learn of your long-standing support of the San Diego Padres and of your many remarkable contributions to our community. On behalf of the entire Padres organization, I would like to thank you for your loyalty. Clearly, you give special meaning to the notion of "keeping the faith."
>
> We are also aware that you have been a bit under the weather of late. But the good news is that you have completed your spell in the hospital and are

> resting comfortably back at home. You have our best wishes for a speedy and complete recovery,
>
> Please know that the Padres will recognize your many contributions to the San Diego community on both radio and on our Sony Jumbo Tron during the upcoming Atlanta Braves series …
>
> Thanks once again for being such a superb Padres fan.

Eileen was delighted to receive that letter, and to be honored by her beloved Padres, and she was ecstatic when, in September, they became the 1996 champions of the National League West.

*

Eileen found other pleasures to enjoy that year. She liked to take rides. Tom and I drove her around San Diego many times in 1996. She exclaimed over the lavender jacaranda trees that bloomed on so many of the city's streets in May. She pointed out the house she had lived in on Essex Street, where Everett had first come to call. She exclaimed some more over the new downtown buildings she saw.

"Everett didn't like progress, you know," she said, "but my father was a builder, and oh, how he would have loved San Diego now!"

Eileen also liked to look out the studio window of her home. She was fascinated by the trolley tracks that were slowly appearing in the valley below.

"When the trolleys start running down there," she said, "I want to ride on one. That's what I want to do on my next birthday, if they're ready by then. I also want to see what's happening down there. There seems to be a lot of building going on." She thought for a second and added, "And sometime this winter I'd like to go up to the top of that hotel you pointed out to me downtown. Then I can get a real view of San Diego and see what else is new."

Eileen did not get to take that ride, or go up to the top of the Hyatt Hotel, for she died on November 25, 1996. Although it is sad that she never rode the trolley or saw the view from the Hyatt, I think the important thing to remember is that she was looking forward to both experiences and was making definite plans. She remained true to her nature to the very end.

The reporter in her was curious about the activity in the valley and in the downtown area. The adventurer in her was eager to visit the Top of the Hyatt and to get on one of those trolleys. In her last year of life, much of her past had faded from her memory. But to reporters and adventurers, the future matters more than the past. In the fall of 1996 Eileen was thinking about her city, and, as always, she was looking ahead.